SECOND EDITION

Different Brains, Different Learners

SECOND EDITION

Different Brains, Different Learners

How to Reach the Hard to Reach

Eric
JENSEN

CORWIN

A SAGE Company

For information:

Corwin
A SAGE Company
2455 Teller Road
Thousand Oaks, California 91320
(800) 233-9936
Fax: (800) 417-2466
www.corwinpress.com

SAGE Ltd.
1 Oliver's Yard
55 City Road
London EC1Y 1SP
United Kingdom

SAGE India Pvt. Ltd.
B 1/I 1 Mohan Cooperative
    Industrial Area
Mathura Road, New Delhi 110 044
India

SAGE Asia-Pacific Pte. Ltd.
33 Pekin Street #02-01
Far East Square
Singapore 048763

Library of Congress Cataloging-in-Publication Data

Jensen, Eric, 1950-
Different brains, different learners : how to reach the hard to reach / Eric P. Jensen.—2nd ed.
    p. cm.
Includes bibliographical references and index.
ISBN 978-1-4129-6501-9 (cloth)
ISBN 978-1-4129-6502-6 (pbk.)
    1. Learning disabled children—Education. 2. Attention-deficit disordered children—Education. 3. Dyslexic children—Education. 4. Learning disabilities. I. Title.

LC4704.J46 2010
371.9—dc22   2009027818

This book is printed on acid-free paper.

09   10   11   12   13   10   9   8   7   6   5   4   3   2   1

Acquisitions Editor:	Carol Chambers Collins
Editorial Assistant:	Brett Ory
Production Editor:	Cassandra Margaret Seibel
Copy Editor:	Sarah J. Duffy
Typesetter:	C&M Digitals (P) Ltd.
Proofreader:	Susan Schon
Indexer:	Sheila Bodell
Cover Designer:	Rose Storey
Graphic Designer:	Lisa Riley

Contents

Preface

Over the years, I've enjoyed enthusiastic feedback from many teachers who have used my earlier books. But the fact is, those books were written for the majority of students—those for whom simply smarter teaching strategies can make the difference. What about the students who don't respond positively even in well-managed learning environments? I can't tell you how many times I've heard teachers ask, "But what about students who . . . ?"

Students who succeed at school need a "good enough" brain. This concept means that a student does not need to have a genius IQ, but does need to have enough mental subskills and the proper attitude to create success. For example, when a student underperforms, it may not be due to attitude; instead it may be the package of subskills that is underperforming (e.g., weaker attentional skills regulated by the frontal lobes). The academic skill package may also include sequencing and processing, which are guided by the parietal, temporal, and frontal lobes. The beauty of understanding these cerebral systems is that you can narrow your efforts to the things that will give you the biggest return on your time and money.

We know where in the brain attention is processed and which skills can enhance it at school. For example, specific art programs (e.g., music, dance, visual arts) can build attentional skills. The larger picture is that brains can change, but first you need to know where and how to do it in a school context. This book introduces you to the what, where, and how of changing the brain in a positive way.

As I've said many times, healthy brains make healthy learners. And with healthy learners and a positive learning environment, you have a good shot at high achievement scores. But what happens when a learner is exposed to chronic stress, trauma, or drugs? What happens when a student's brain is impacted by developmental delays, abnormality, or chemical imbalances? Quite simply, you need better resources to succeed. A brain-based approach is guided by the brain's understanding of function, structure, systems, and processes. This may be a better way because it can help you target your efforts.

HOW TO USE THIS NEW EDITION

Different Brains, Different Learners is a practical, comprehensive survey that tells you in plain language how to recognize the most common conditions that challenge learners and how to help them succeed. This book is not about all learners who fall through the cracks, only the most common. Even if *Different Brains, Different Learners* were three times as long, it would still be difficult to explore each condition that impacts students today. Every kind of learner passes through our classroom doors, and every one of them deserves to succeed.

While some learners will improve academically and behaviorally merely through your recognition, caring, and outreach, others will require therapeutic interventions and interdisciplinary care. In either case, there is hope. There are no unreachable students. And once you master these skills and strategies, your once borderline students can succeed. Isn't that what teaching is all about?

Perhaps the greatest concern among educators at the moment is the disproportionate class time used to produce higher test scores—a present-day dilemma that can mean less attention to individualized instruction, life skills, the arts, and reaching troubled learners. But there is a deeper question we should be asking: What will prepare learners most for life success—higher test scores or a well-rounded education? What business are we in—the information business or the people business? I say we're in the people business!

Can we do both? Can we groom a child for life success and achieve higher test scores? Yes! But our priority must be clear. If we focus first on people, we can trust that tests scores will ultimately improve. But if we focus first on testing, we can expect that learners will undoubtedly suffer—especially the ones who need us most.

With *Different Brains, Different Learners* you'll become better equipped to successfully identify and address the learning impairments that are so common today, yet often neglected in teacher education programs. It is easy to feel overwhelmed when you think of implementing all the strategies in this book. But relax and take one step at a time. Ultimately, you will become a much more efficient, effective, and rewarded teacher of diverse learners.

With your increased awareness, you'll spend less time and energy on problems you can't control, you'll minimize disruptions to the rest of the class, you'll learn how to accommodate various disorders, and you'll understand when it is important to refer a student out for expert consultation. All of us already work hard, so working harder is not the answer. We have to work smarter. Remember: you make a difference, and you change lives. Go on and do what you do best. And most important, enjoy the challenge!

Acknowledgments

C orwin gratefully acknowledges the contributions of the following reviewers:

Mary Beth Cary, Teacher
Worth County Primary School
Sylvester, GA

Gerard A. Dery, Principal
Nessacus Regional Middle School, NAESP Board, Zone 1 Director
Dalton, MA

John La Londe, SELPA Director
Marin SELPA
San Rafael, CA

Debra Paradowski, Administrator
Arrowhead Union High School
Hartland, WI

About the Author

 **Eric Jensen** is a former teacher with a real love of learning. He has taught at all levels, from elementary through university, and is currently completing his PhD in human development. In 1981, Jensen cofounded SuperCamp (Quantum Learning), the nation's first and largest brain-compatible learning program, now with over fifty thousand graduates. He has since written *Super Teaching, Teaching With the Brain in Mind, Brain-Based Learning, Enriching the Brain,* and 25 other books on learning and the brain. A leader in the brain-based movement, Jensen has made over 65 visits to neuroscience labs and interacts with dozens of neuroscientists annually.

Jensen is currently an active member of the Society for Neuroscience and the New York Academy of Sciences. He was the founder of the Learning Brain EXPO and has trained educators and trainers for 25 years worldwide in this field. He is deeply committed to making a positive, significant, lasting difference in the way we learn. Currently, Jensen does conference speaking, in-school staff development, and in-depth trainings on engagement, enriching students from poverty and student achievement. Go to www.jensenlearning.com or e-mail his wife Diane at diane@jlcbrain.com.

Introduction

10 TRUTHS BEFORE YOU BEGIN

1 There is considerable comorbidity (overlap) in these disorders. A single disorder is truly the exception. In this book, each chapter takes on a disorder for the sake of convenience. Most commonly there are at least two, sometimes three, disorders present at the same time. Students who are oppositional are also highly likely to have attention deficit hyperactivity disorder. Remember, everything in the brain is connected to something else.

2 It's likely that all of these disorders are multicausal. Nevertheless, likely causes are listed separately in this book for the sake of clarity. Most of the time, the cause is a combination of genetics and environment, because those two interact in complex ways. Typically, multiple factors—a genetic mutation or susceptibility, childhood neglect, toxins, malnutrition, abuse, and/or prenatal trauma—are implicated. A traumatic life event or prolonged exposure to stress contributes to the problem.

3 There are multiple models (and each accurate!) for understanding these disorders. Models come from the fields of psychiatry, pediatric neurology, special education, and cutting-edge neuroscience. For example, some educators treat classroom discipline as a maturity issue or a self-control issue. Others treat it as a social or even medical issue. Just remember that there are many ways to solve the same problems.

4 There is no single location in the brain for a disorder. The specific locations identified in this book offer a simple glimpse of some areas that are likely impacted. Nearly every neurological event is system driven in ways that impact many areas of the brain. For example, social skills require more than paying attention; you have to pay attention to the relevant facial and vocal messages, or you'll miss the real meaning. Remember, there are no isolated neurological events; instead, there are regulatory systems with identifiable pathways.

5 There is no doubt more to learn about these disorders. Much greater study is needed. Brain-imaging technology is new and amazing, but it should never be the only source of information. We will see the accuracy improve, the functionality increase, and the costs go down. Hand-held brain scanners are already being used. Consider this book as "Here's what we know so far."

6 Every learner can learn and improve. The human brain is designed to respond to environmental input: the more targeted, persistent, and relevant the input, the greater the changes. To get the changes you want, first learn about which systems you want to target. It's all a matter of resources (e.g., time, personnel, technology, medication, support). Make the commitment to ensure that all students have a fighting chance.

7 Avoid perfectionism; it will rob you of the potential for gratifying rewards. Learn about one disorder at a time, and practice identifying specific learners. This book wasn't written in a day, and you don't need to memorize it in a day in order to receive value from it. One chapter a week, or a month, is all you need. Just keep at it.

8 Look for students' strengths. Not every learner can become excellent in everything. There are significant genetic and environmental variations in the human species.

9 Attitude and knowledge are equally important. Your belief in the highest possibilities of each learner and your capacity to identify symptoms and activate appropriate responses and resources are the most important variables in learner success. Students will pick up on your positive attitude and find hope within it.

10 Take pride in everyday successes, whether large or small. Learners learn much more from who you are than from what you teach. Maybe your biggest gift is caring and doing your best. Never underestimate the power of hope and compassionate relationships or the value of implicit learning and positive role modeling.

Pretest

CAN YOU IDENTIFY THESE LEARNERS?

Learner No. 1: Miguel

Symptoms

♦ Loses his temper often

♦ Argues with adults; defies authority and rejects adults' requests or rules; complies about 10 to 20 percent of the time

♦ Deliberately annoys others and is easily annoyed himself

♦ Blames others for his own mistakes or misbehavior

♦ Angry and resentful; vindictive for no apparent reason

♦ Swears and uses obscene language

Miguel is fourteen years old and smart. He's managed to get just about everyone in class mad at him. What's most likely going on?

Answer: _____

Learner No. 2: Tom

Symptoms

♦ Displays a high level of apathy, listlessness, or lack of vigor

♦ Passive and unresponsive in spite of shocking or surprising events

♦ Does not initiate new activities or learning

♦ Does not feel in control of his environment; likely to say, "What's the point?," "Why bother?," "Who cares?," or "So what?"

♦ Lack of hostility even when hostility is warranted

♦ Increased sarcasm

Tom is 21 years old. He attends adult school because if he doesn't he will be kicked out of his house. The above symptoms have continued for about three to four months. His teacher can't quite nail down what's wrong. What's most likely going on?

Answer: _____

Learner No. 3: Joshua

Symptoms

- Inappropriate emotional outbursts with random acts of destruction
- Consistently hurtful toward peers—swatting, hitting, and verbal intimidation
- Refuses to follow directions directly; consistently challenges authority
- Loud and aggressive communication patterns, often taunting the teacher and using vulgar language
- Unwilling to participate with others in normal social activities
- Is prone to lie

This pattern began in first grade and has continued into high school. What's most likely going on?

Answer: _____

Learner No. 4: Mary

Symptoms

- Seems to be edgy and on alert
- Trance-like state is common; doesn't snap out of it quickly
- Appears bored and disconnected
- Short-term memory loss and inability to prioritize
- Makes careless errors in her work
- Decreased social contact
- Doesn't remember "where" questions
- Loss of creativity and poor concentration
- Seems to be sick more often than peers

Mary, a high-school student, is struggling when, just a few years prior, she seemed so enthusiastic. Now it seems she is in a trance all the time. What's most likely going on?

Answer: _____

Learner No. 5: Michelle

Symptoms

♦ Decrease in energy
♦ Change in appetite and subsequent weight loss or gain
♦ Feelings of worthlessness and guilt
♦ Inability to think clearly or concentrate; indecisiveness
♦ Angry, sometimes suicidal imaginings
♦ Persistent sad, anxious, or empty mood
♦ Feelings of hopelessness; pessimism
♦ Loss of interest or pleasure in ordinary activities or hobbies
♦ Restlessness, irritability, unexplained aches and pains
♦ Unusual loss of friends; reduction in academic performance

Michelle is a second grader who did well last year. This year her mother is being treated for cancer. What's most likely going on?

Answer: _____

Learner No. 6: Robert

Symptoms

♦ Stays to himself
♦ Often gets stuck and repeats behaviors
♦ Seems obsessed with details
♦ Dislikes changes of routines or surprises
♦ Makes little or no eye contact
♦ Gets sick more often than others
♦ Misses the big picture
♦ Shows fascination over apparent trivia

Robert has had these problems for years. In spite of this, he has been passed from one teacher to the next. What's most likely going on?

Answer: _____

Learner No. 7: Ashley

Symptoms

◆ Difficulty structuring work time
◆ Impaired rates of learning and poor memory
◆ Has trouble generalizing behaviors and information
◆ Sometimes exhibits impulsive behavior
◆ Easily distracted and frequently exhibits reduced attention span
◆ Displays a sense of fearlessness; is unresponsive to verbal cautions
◆ Displays poor social judgment
◆ Has trouble internalizing modeled behaviors
◆ Language production is higher than comprehension
◆ Overall poor problem-solving strategies
◆ May have unusual facial features

Ashley has had these problems for years. In spite of this, she has been passed from one teacher to the next. What's most likely going on?

Answer: _____

Learner No. 8: Courtney

Symptoms

◆ Has difficulty with number and order sequences
◆ Understands the importance of working left to right
◆ Finds telling the time on an analogue clock difficult
◆ Scatters tally marks instead of organizing them systematically
◆ Gets confused with division (e.g., is it 3 into 6, or 6 into 3?)
◆ Gets easily overloaded by pages/worksheets full of figures
◆ Makes copies of work/shapes inaccurately

Courtney has exhibited this behavior pattern from a very early age. She seems to be on high power, while everyone else is operating at normal speed. What's most likely going on?

Answer: _____

Learner No. 9: Brent

Symptoms

- Inattentive to others
- Easily distracted
- Engages in a lot of head turning to hear better
- Retrieval problems ("Um . . . I forget the word.")
- Difficulty following oral directions
- Omits word endings
- Speaks words out of order
- Mistaken words—says "starvation army" instead of Salvation Army or "fum" instead of thumb

This pattern began early, before Brent entered school. He's in the third grade, doing poorly, and he has not been tested. What's most likely going on?

Answer: _____

Learner No. 10: Jason

Symptoms

- Rarely finishes his work
- Calls out answers in class; never waits his turn
- Easily and consistently distracted
- Exhibits weak follow-through and preparation for future events
- Wants everything right away; has no patience
- Personal area (desk) is a mess
- Doesn't seem able to reflect on the past in order to learn from it
- Doesn't sit still; always on the go
- Can't hold several thoughts at a time
- Hindsight or foresight is rarely evident

Jason is a second-grade student with plenty of enthusiasm. He gets average grades. What's most likely going on?

Answer: _____

Learner No. 11: Lee

Symptoms

- Has trouble with sequencing, prioritizing, and completing tasks
- Takes spoken or written language literally
- Has difficulty following oral directions and remembering them
- Inability to rhyme by age four
- Confuses left and right, over and under, before and after, and other directionality words and concepts
- Lack of dominant handedness; switches hands between or even during tasks
- Unable to correctly complete phonemic awareness tasks
- Has difficulty learning the names and sounds of letters and writing them in alphabetical order

Lee, a fifth grader, likes to read but struggles to maintain average grades. He rarely completes his assignments. What's most likely going on?

Answer: _____

Each chapter addresses a different type of learner. Once you finish reading this book, quiz yourself again with the posttest. Meanwhile, talk about the material, try it out, work with a study group, and really get it in your body. What you are about to learn will make a dramatic difference in your work. To find the answers to this quiz, continue reading.

1

Understanding Different Brains

Notice the title of this chapter. It sounds so distant and clinical, as if we are talking about someone else's brains. But you and I know it's not the brains of "those" students out there; it's the brains of your own students and maybe even your own children. The reason I used a sort of impersonal format is because, just for a moment, I'd like you to consider the generic three-pound mass on top of your shoulders. Just for a moment, think of the misbehaving or underperforming brain as a mystery to solve instead of as a problem. This chapter puts critical pieces of the puzzle together for you. You may be surprised what has been learned recently about the human brain, behavior, and academic achievement.

THE MYTH OF THE HEALTHY OR "TYPICAL" BRAIN

Intuition tells teachers to use differentiation strategies with their students. If you were to scan the actual structure of the human brain, what would you discover? At the Department of Neurology in the David Geffen School of Medicine at UCLA, neuroscientists have been collecting brain data from around the world as well as using their own state-of-the-art scans. They have scanned the healthy, "normal" human brain throughout the human lifespan using structural and functional brain imaging data. As part of the

International Consortium for Brain Mapping (ICBM), these scientists have developed a set of "normal" criteria for subject inclusion. The idea was to discover what the typical brain looks like. Naturally, they needed the associated exclusion criteria, too.

Over several years, almost 2,000 subjects responded to public advertisements for "those with no health problems." Each of the consortium sites (e.g., UCLA) ensured that every subject was prescreened by (1) a detailed telephone interview, (2) in-person history gathering, and (3) physical examination. This procedure was designed to exclude those who were not likely to have healthy, typical brains. For example, those with a history of head trauma, high blood pressure, violence, and long-term medication usage or drug abuse were excluded from the study.

Let's find out how common it is to have a healthy brain. Of those who responded to the advertisement and considered themselves to be normal, only 32 percent passed the telephone screening process. Of those who qualified for the in-person health history and physical examination, only 52 percent passed these screening procedures. Now we can do the math: only 11 percent of those individuals who believed they were healthy and normal even qualified for imaging. The study concludes by saying, "The majority of individuals who consider themselves normal by self-report are found not to be so" (Mazziotta et al., 2009, p. 914).

What does this tell you about people who are known to have problems, differences, or disabilities? The study suggests reexamining the inclusion of qualifications of subjects in brain imaging studies, the criteria used to select them, and the conclusions that can be drawn from them (Mazziotta et al., 2009). By the way, the study was published in a peer-reviewed scientific journal by pioneers in the brain-imaging field, including John Mazziotta and Arthur Toga. The take-home message from this study is that differences are the norm, not the exception!

Understanding What Runs the Brain

We start with the premise that all brains are unique. Now we acknowledge that children's brains are influenced by a host of factors. They include (but are not limited to) exposure to toxins, genetics, relationships, socioeconomic status, siblings, maternal education, maternal drug abuse, and what mom did during pregnancy. First, different factors have a different influence at different ages. How much your mother (or primary caregiver) lavishes attention on you matters more from birth to age 3 than from, for example, 13 to 15 years old. Peers, on the other hand, mean more to a teenager than they do to a 2-year-old. Teens want social status more than kids do at age 5. Second, at every age there are factors that exacerbate others and cause outcomes to deteriorate. If you don't have friends at age 12 but you excel at sports, you may avoid depression. If you don't get a quality childcare experience but your childhood included a wide range of engaging, age-appropriate activities, you may have no disadvantage.

The point here is that your brain develops depending on the aggregate of factors over time. One event (unless it is a significant trauma) is less likely to change the developing brain, but many do over time.

What Matters Most to the Developing Brain

The primary underlying factor beneath everyday experiences that is the foundation for academics, socialization, and achievement is genetics. Genetics contributes to about 30–50 percent of life's outcomes. But genes are not our destiny. Yes, they code for eye, hair, and skin color; a narrow selection of diseases; and various other qualities. But genes are only part of the equation. The two largest parts of the equation are interactions between genes and the environment and everyday experiences. You have undoubtedly heard of the importance of both genetic and environmental factors. The old nature-versus-nurture debates used to pit environmental factors against genes. That's outdated and oversimplified.

Humans share over 99 percent of the same genes. Yet within any two humans (think of your students), the precise identical shared genes may be expressed in one and not in another. Gene expression is the capacity of the environment to influence genetic messages via an "on/off" switch that tells genes to make proteins (or not). Genetic expression is much of the reason that family members of even identical twins can share the same DNA and yet still have a very different personality. In fact, most of the personality differences within a family or ethnicity (with both shared genes and culture) are a result of gene expression. This is a huge source of differentiation among humans. What activates the switching is a wide array of factors. You'll be introduced to them later, but they include social conditions, exercise, new learning, stress, and environments.

So what does all this mean in the context of our discussion of how to understand the brain? It means that genes are just part of the equation. The expression "the apple doesn't fall far from the tree" is outdated, wrong, and damaging. Sometimes apples do fall far from the tree. For example, a pair of identical conjoined twins, joined at the brain at birth, lived the first 29 years of their life attached, experiencing every one of life's moments together—sleeping, eating, learning, illness, and so on. Their genes and experiences would suggest that these two people would be alike. Yet they had two very different personalities. Genes are not our destiny. And that means other factors will influence how your students turn out. The question is: Can you apply positive factors purposely and quickly so that your students will have a fighting chance to succeed in life?

Keep in mind that all brains develop with an everyday working platform. In healthy learners, both emotionally and academically this platform supports the behaviors that lead to good grades and social skills. But in students who struggle, their platform is overwhelmed by risk factors (see Figure 1.1), which are built on genetic scaffolding and exacerbated by adverse life experiences. The aggregate of risk factors for those with academic or social impairment can be small or huge. On a behavioral level, it could range from mild attention deficit hyperactivity disorder to severe conduct disorder. On the academic level, it could vary from a child with treatable dyslexia to one with severe autism. We've all seen how risk factors can be dominant in a child's life. An example would be a child with significant learning delays; the brain's platform for school success is compromised.

Figure 1.1   An Impaired Operating System

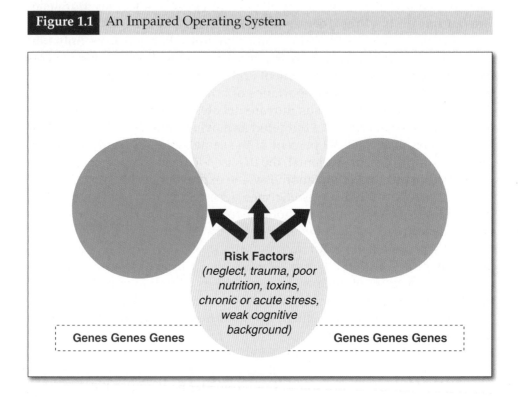

Risk Factors Can Seem Overwhelming

In a perfect world, all children would arrive at school with workable academic and social operating systems, ready to be fine-tuned by a positive school experience. Unfortunately, not all children have a malleable yet undamaged operating system (i.e., the brain's way of getting through the experience at hand) that is ready for school. That's what this book is all about. When children have been exposed to adverse life experiences without the coping skills to survive or thrive, their operating system or the capacity to build it may be compromised. What might compromise the healthy development of a child's operating system for successful school behaviors or academics? Here are some factors:

- exposure to neglect or abuse
- parents who are divorced or separated

- exposure to toxins (e.g., lead, pesticides)
- insufficient exposure to complex language
- head injury
- prenatal exposure to alcohol
- chronic or acute stress
- lack of healthy exploratory play
- chronic inner ear infections

Now, using the platform in Figure 1.1, the genetic factors would still be the underpinnings, but the primary driver in student performance would be risk (versus success) factors. That may not be fair, but it's the reality. In addition, a student's operating system may simply be underdeveloped through neglect or ignorance. Some parents may not know what it takes to raise children or get them "school ready." There's nothing hardwired in parents that tell them to do the right things in raising a child, aside from being protective. Outside of that protectiveness, many environmental factors come into play. The stronger the operating system, the greater a student's capacity to overcome severe adversity (risk factors).

We each have many operating systems, each of which contains various subskills for a different situation. We might show an operating system graphically like this:

Figure 1.2   Our Platform Is an Operating System

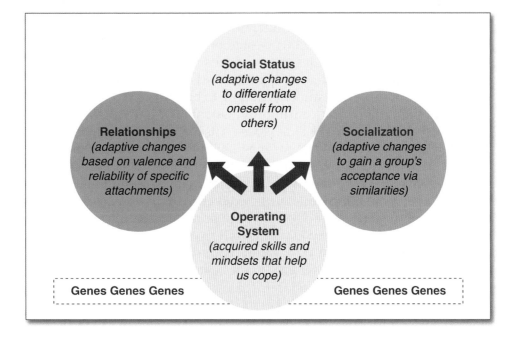

A bit later on, we'll fill in the other circles. For now, what actually is the operating system? It is a brain system comprising subsystems that are context dependent. For example, you have a survival-oriented operating system that lets you focus in an emergency on the fewest possible variables from one moment to the next and exclude trivia (e.g., a sore toe, an e-mail to answer, the fact that you are mad at your sister). This particular operating system is not in effect all the time unless you live in extreme conditions such as a war zone, abuse, or severe poverty. You have other overlapping operating systems, including a social one and a professional one, that you use more often. Even children have various operating systems, but theirs are quite raw and undeveloped depending on their age and life experiences.

This academic operating system is not inclusive of everything kids need in life. Our brains develop other operating systems for socialization, survival, jobs, and a host of other behaviorally relevant needs. The academic operating system does not include love, sacrifice, duty, fairness, humor, kindness, and a host of other values. But to succeed in school, a champion's mind set, hope, attentional skills, memory, processing, and sequencing skills are must-haves. These are highly leveragable, critically needed skill sets. The good news is that these subsystems (e.g., attention) that comprise the aggregate operating system can be taught!

Students are not stuck the way they are. Their success is dependent on their operating system, and it can be upgraded. For example, physical activity can increase a student's production of new brain cells (Pereira et al., 2007), and this is highly correlated with learning, mood, and memory. Playing chess can increase reading (Margulies, 1991) and math (Cage & Smith, 2000) capabilities by increasing attention, motivation, processing, and sequencing skills. Using certain computer-aided instructional programs can, in just weeks, increase attention and improve working memory (Kerns, McInerney, & Wilde, 2001; Westerberg & Klingberg, 2007), both of which are significant upgrades to a student's operating system. Students are not stuck with poor attention span. Instead of demanding more attention in class, you can train students in how to build it.

In addition, many arts can improve attentional and cognitive skills (Posner, Rothbart, Sheese, & Kieras, 2008). Arts can also upgrade the system by teaching sequencing and processing skills. To put it bluntly, building capacity to learn (i.e., upgrading the operating system) is much more important than adding more content, and for many reasons. One of them is that you get more return on your time investment. If you fail to plan an upgrade for the skills your students need in order to learn and process academic information, you are planning to fail.

You can mitigate many risk factors with a strong operating system. Without improvements in their processing capacity, students' achievement will stagnate. An old Commodore 64 computer had so little processing power that no matter how fast you typed or how much content you had, it still tended to overwhelm the system. Raising standards and having high expectations is admirable. But wishing and hoping something dramatic will happen is not enough. You've got to enable and build the brain's operating system to make progress happen. Whatever you did in the past that worked, it upgraded students' operating systems. Every successful school intervention for kids from low-income neighborhoods features a variation on the theme of rebuilding the operating system. This system works on the principle of using the fewest processes that matter most to the learning process. If you simply try to cram more content into the same brain without upgrading the operating system, students will get bored, become frustrated, and fail. Good interventions build effective systems. Each day, our brains adapt to our experiences, and this newly changing brain influences us. There's a chicken-and-egg effect happening: we change our brains, and our changed brains then change us.

In a school situation, the operating system comprises two of the four parts of the big picture: hope and the skills needed. To this we add the final pieces: accommodations and enrichment. We now have a "sea of hope" for students (see Figure 1.3).

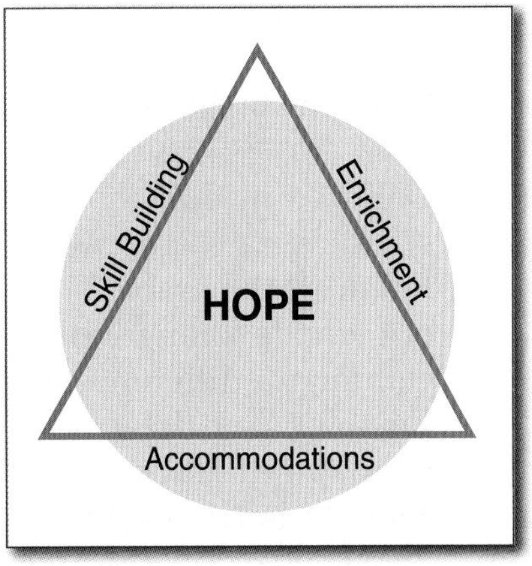

While being hopeful and building skills, we must also balance students' needs for accommodations and enrichment. When educators use accommodations appropriately, they help level the playing field. Enrichment overcomes many problems and challenges in the brain because of the brain's capacity to change for the better. Enrichment has been shown to overcome the effects of learning delays, memory loss, attachment disorders, fetal alcoholism, and drug abuse. When we bring together skill building, enrichment, accommodations, and hope, we get a powerful plan that accelerates the chances for success.

Figure 1.3   A Sea of Hope

With each of the challenges discussed in this book comes a different balance of what's needed to maximize change in the brain. In some cases, hope is most critical. In others, skill building will solve most of the issues. Each chapter offers a practical plan to use for student success, and each plan includes many suggestions that you can use immediately. The theme of the suggestions is building students' operating systems. Without that focus, students will not have a good chance to succeed. You are about to embark on a wonderful journey to change your students' brains.

2

The Brain's Key Operating Systems

This book sets up what educators call "differences" in kids. There are primarily two different categories, or operating systems, explored in this book: social and academic. The framework for understanding each empowers you as the educator to think about what is different in the brain. This operating system model is less about figuring out what's wrong with a "broken" brain and more about simply understanding a differences model that needs to work well in the context of school. As we delve into these differences, you will see that there is little overlap in the specific subskills of each operating system. But the basic concept is the same—when this system is impaired, the student has problems.

THE BRAIN'S SOCIAL OPERATING SYSTEM

A child's social-emotional operating system is actually quite complex. In fact, you could dream up quite a long list of attitudes, skills, and so on that students need to have in order to socialize properly in school, some of which can be taught quickly or managed through socialization (e.g., waiting their turn in line, keeping their hands off others, responding to social cues with appropriate behavior). But only a few core skills are needed to succeed.

The Social Brain Can Be Rewired With Experience

While many areas of the brain are involved in social capacities, we'll focus on six primary systems: sensory awareness, social reasoning, theory of mind, affiliation and empathy, emotional states, and reward evaluation (see Figure 2.1). When you build the subskills of these systems, you strengthen the brain in ways that will provide lasting gifts. These subskills truly enable students to get a leg up in life because good social skills are high on the list of what matters most.

The relevance of understanding these subskills is simple: when students have social and behavioral issues, one or more of these six factors is not up to the level needed to succeed in school. That does not mean the student is "broken." It simply means that one of the contributing brain patterns of social success is not working well for success in a school environment. For example, many adults with high-functioning Asperger syndrome can do quite well finding a job and earning a living in society, but kids with this syndrome struggle in a school-based environment that is highly cooperative because their brains don't process social information well. This does not mean, however, that they can't succeed in school. They have a different brain, not a broken one. Most gaps can be filled, and new skills can be learned. It simply takes understanding and patience. All kids can learn; educators must have the will, time, and the resources to make that happen.

Figure 2.1 The Brain's Social Operating System

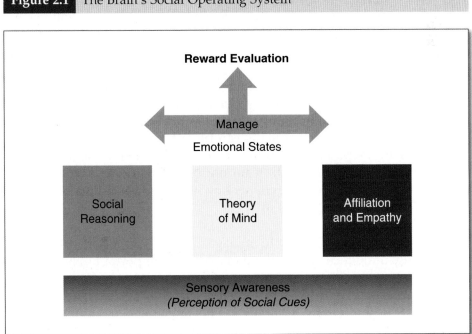

When any part of this operating system is not functioning well, there are various strategies you can use to strengthen it. (See Table 2.1 also, for resources to consult for additional ideas.)

Sensory Awareness. This area deals with perception and accurate processing of relevant social cues. Develop these skills through role-plays, direct instruction, and follow-up discussion.

STRATEGIES: In class, use case studies of common student scenarios and engage students in cooperative small-group work to teach them to think differently about how to behave. Watch a DVD as a class, and discuss what happened and what could be done different.

Social Reasoning. This involves the capacity to make decisions with others in mind, gain acceptance within a given group, and manage the effects of peer pressure.

STRATEGIES: Teach listening skills explicitly as part of a cooperative learning activity. Students need to be part of a well-defined and well-managed cooperative group to hear and see the effects of social behaviors and participate in developing social reasoning skills. Use case studies for older kids (Grades 5 and up). Use direct instruction coaching with all ages.

Theory of Mind. This is the capacity to put oneself in another's shoes in order to predict that person's likely actions and feel empathy for him or her.

STRATEGIES: This set of subskills can be enhanced by prediction activities in language arts and partner work that require students to make assumptions. Role-plays and case studies of highly typical student behaviors and scenarios are another great source for learning to predict another's mind set.

Affiliation and Empathy. These skills are defined by reliable, relational bonding with another person. Many students with disorders related to this area have had chaotic upbringings with insecure or hostile attachments.

STRATEGIES: This set of skills can be enhanced by experience and feedback with cooperative learning, teams, and other close-knit group time. It must be reinforced with team norms, feedback, and both teacher and peer assessments. Teach students how to form friendships and, more important, how to maintain them.

Emotional States. The capacity to manage one's own emotional states and purposefully influence those of others is very important. This can be developed best through long-term activities that have a chance to gain student interest and showcase varied responses.

STRATEGIES: Options for training the brain include drama, theater groups, role-plays, and writing fiction stories about people's lives. In addition, sports can help students learn to manage the feelings of winning and losing and recognize the value of good sportsmanship.

Reward Evaluation. This is the adaptive use of reciprocity—appropriate responsiveness to social signals with a healthy give and take. Positive social interactions can be very emotionally rewarding. But this is learned; it is not innate in the brain's wiring. The teacher needs to take a strong role here. Unless students have learned to get positive feelings from "please" and "thank you" as well as a host of other social cues such as handshakes, and hugs, it will be foreign to them.

STRATEGIES: Teach healthy give-and-take responses in class, and model them for all of your students. Don't tell students what to do; show them *how* to do it. This is typically modeled in the healthy family. Without that modeling at home, students can still learn it through classroom activities such as writing letters of gratitude to others.

As one might expect, many educators have difficulty teaching social skills to school-age children. Part of it is that the process is time intensive. It is also very different than teaching definitions, numbers, letters, or days of the week. There are multiple components, including syntax (the rules of language), semantics (the nonverbals and meaning behind actual words), and pragmatics (the situational use of social language). Without each part functioning, there will be difficulties. And it takes each of the six previously discussed parts of the model to ensure proper functioning. Otherwise, one cannot be a successful and complete communicator.

Table 2.1   Building Social Skills

Web Sites for Building Social Skills

Let's Face It! web.uvic.ca/~jtanaka/letsfaceit/activities.php

Posit Science Cortex, www.positscience.com

Social Skill Builder, www.socialskillbuilder.com/howtochoose.html

Second Life, secondlife.com

Longer-Term, In-Depth Programs to Build Social Skills

TeachTown.com

Natural Environment Teaching (NET)

Pivotal Response Training (PRT)

Prelinguistic Milieu Teaching (PMT)

Boardmaker

Laureate Learning Systems

SpeechTeach

Picture This

What you'll notice in the strategies offered in the next several chapters is that every one of them relates to these six core skills. These six skills are presented first because they provide the framework for understanding the rest of the strategies. For example, many students have a tough time being social or civil the moment stress levels go up, and students with oppositional disorder are among those most behaviorally challenged by increased stress. The emotional states factor discussed earlier speaks to this challenge. Only by learning stress-reducing strategies (e.g., reframing, taking deep breaths, seeing another's point of view, counting to 20) will students ever have a chance to get their lives back under control.

How to Maximize Results

Building the social operating system is a top priority. If a student is in an impoverished home environment for hours every day and then gets a few minutes of operating system enhancement at school, that time constitutes only a tiny fragment of the student's total week. That time is unlikely to produce substantial long-term benefits (though it's certainly better than nothing). The message here is clear: do not kid yourself about changing the brain—it takes time.

The human brain is highly susceptible to environmental input. In some cases, change—even permanent change—can happen within minutes. But that's likely to be a change induced by trauma (e.g., emotional, psychological, physical). To get lasting positive change, you'll want to go right up to the maximum time per day allowed by the brain, which on average is about 30 to 90 minutes of intensive skill building in any area. Beyond that, there's no evidence of gain. The brain just overloads, and the change is dismissed.

Let's translate this into your school time. To maximize change with skill building, students will have to be in a pullout situation. Why? Unless one follows the brain's rules for skill building, precious time is wasted, students learn less, and teachers get frustrated. The rules are simple (see Table 2.2).

However, as Chapter 1 revealed, there are other ways to get improvement without direct instruction in skill building. You can place a student in an enrichment (i.e., inclusion) classroom, but this is only valuable if two things take place: there is also pullout time for skill building each day, and the student is not highly disruptive to the class. In addition, you can facilitate growth indirectly through accommodations. This four-part system from Chapter 1 is repeated here because it is so powerful:

1. Always provide hope.

2. Organize as much skill building for the operating system as you can.

3. Create enrichment opportunities whenever possible.

4. Ensure that any needed accommodations are made.

Table 2.2   Skill-Building Rules

Learner must:

Buy into an activity

Perceive relevance

Get good sleep

Have focused attention

Activity must:

Be coherent to learners

Build in both positive and
negative feedback

Last 30 to 90 minutes a day

Occur three to six times per week

Even if the conditions, resources, or policies are not ideal, take and use any of the suggested interventions that you can. The optimal ones, the ones that accelerate progress, use all four of these factors. The best interventions build an operating system because that's the most lasting change and it ripples across all areas of one's life.

THE BRAIN'S ACADEMIC OPERATING SYSTEM

Academic skills have a brain system that overlaps with social skills in the areas of awareness and attention. It's not a huge overlap, but there are some connections nonetheless. At school, the primary factors that interact, mitigate, or support the academic operating system are relationships, socialization, and social status. Each of these plays a part in the motivation, decision making, and cognition needed to succeed each day.

Students do not need to be superior in all of these areas to get good grades, but they do need enough of any compensatory strategies to succeed. The good news is that each of the critical processes in the brain's academic operating system is malleable, trainable, and can be improved.

The CHAMPS Mind Set

To make the brain system more memorable, I have labeled the academic operating system CHAMPS, an acronym that refers to a champion's mind set, hope, attention, memory, processing, and sequencing (see Figure 2.2).

Figure 2.2 The Brain's Academic Operating System

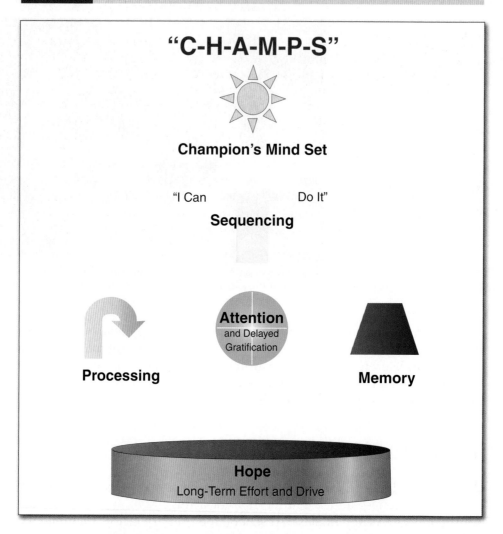

Let's consolidate what we know. Students are not stuck the way they are. Their success is dependent on their operating system, and it can be upgraded. For example, physical activity can increase a student's production of new brain cells (Pereira et al., 2007), and this is highly correlated with learning, mood, and memory. Playing chess can increase reading (Margulies, 1991) and math (Cage & Smith, 2000) capabilities by increasing attention, motivation, processing, and sequencing skills. Many arts can improve attentional and cognitive skills (Posner, Rothbart, Sheese, & Kieras, 2008). Using certain computer-aided instructional programs can, in just weeks, increase attention and improve working memory (Kerns, McInerney, & Wilde, 2001; Westerberg & Klingberg, 2007), both of which are significant upgrades to a student's operating system. Students are not stuck with poor attention span. Instead of demanding more attention in class, you can train students in how to build it with the following strategies.

Champion's Mind Set. This is the way of thinking that exudes confidence.

STRATEGIES: Give students genuine affirmations often, and support deserving student-to-student affirmations. Provide support for learning with tools, partners, and confidence. Create short assignments and opportunities for quick successes that tell the learners, "You can do it!" Help strengthen their social status by providing appropriate opportunities for privileges with their peers.

Hope. Hope is the voice that says, "There are better days ahead." It is fundamental for long-term effort. It requires deferred gratification and only works when there is something to be hopeful for. Students who have learned helplessness have a complete lack of hope, as do many with learning delays. But you can help change this.

STRATEGIES: Strengthen teacher-to-student relationships so that students know they have social support. Create situations in which students can experience success. Provide quality role models for success. Teach imagination, positive goal setting, and how to achieve those goals. Help students learn to manage their time and create checklists to manage their lives. Teach them how to make better choices, and give them practice at making choices. Ask them about their dreams, and let them draw, sing, talk, write, or rap about them.

Attentional Skills and Delayed Gratification. Paying attention is not an innate skill. What's innate is shifting attention from one novel attention grabber to another. It takes practice to learn to focus on the details over time. Students with attention deficit problems typically have focus and attention issues (among others).

STRATEGIES: Focus on high-interest arts content that allows students to immerse themselves in a situation requiring detailed focus. Build focus through high-interest reading. Build attention through focused practice in martial arts, dance, chess, model building, and sports. Helpful Web sites include fitbrains.com and playattention.com.

Memory. In school, a strong memory is not just expected, it is priceless. We are born with a good long-term memory for spatial learning, emotional events, procedural and skill learning, conditioned response learning, and highly behaviorally relevant data such as our phone number and the names of our siblings and parents. Outside of these, school learning requires both short-term memory and long-term faculties.

STRATEGIES: Practice with simple call-and-response in class. Build up to pair-share with partners. Strengthen memory with repetition, framing the importance of an idea. Teach students memory aids (e.g., mnemonics, loci method, peg systems, acronyms). Develop their skills in mind mapping.

Processing. This is the capacity to flesh something out. At the micro level, it means a student can process auditory input such as phonemes, which is quite important for reading. At the macro level, it means a student can process an event (e.g., being called a name, breaking up with a lover, forgetting to do homework). We all need to know how to deal with difficulties, particularly emotional ones. And we need to be able to ask appropriate questions and think critically about a problem. Kids with dyslexia or learning delays often have significant processing issues.

STRATEGIES: Provide verbal walk-throughs of class processes (e.g., "Now we are doing this . . . and next we'll need to. . . ."). Teach critical thinking and logic skills (specialized software can help with this). Offer challenging games with structured practice time. Encourage students to play a musical instrument or take drama classes; both will strengthen memory. Give students a partner so they can develop metaskills as they learn to talk through their thinking and acting process.

Sequencing. This is the set of skills that allow us to prioritize, identify, and put in order a set of actions. When you prepare a meal for guests, pack for a trip, or paint a bedroom, you need sequencing skills. At school, kids need these skills for starting homework, writing a paper, planning a project, resolving conflict, doing a math problem, and planning their day.

STRATEGIES: Experience and mentoring are the two best teachers for this skill set. Give students the opportunity to build things (e.g., models, paper projects, displays). Be the guide for each project to help set goals, organize materials, and use preteaching in organizing their work, writing a paper, or problem solving. Encourage them to get involved in the arts; most arts opportunities require attention, hope, processing, and sequencing.

Without an upgrade of these skills, your school will be doing more of the same and getting more of the same. When you upgrade students' systems for learning, you completely change the equation. In this book, you'll learn how to upgrade any student's impaired academic operating system, including those with problems in reading, math, and overall learning delays. When we address academic problems throughout the course of this book, it will always come back to strengthening students' academic operating systems. Stronger systems mean better performance.

3

The Argumentative Learner

Oppositional Defiant Disorder

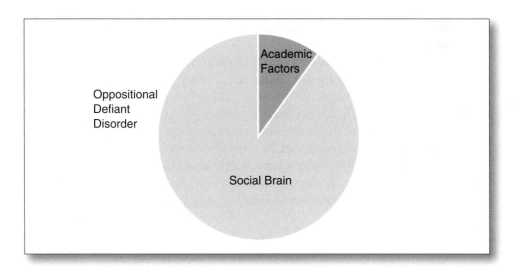

O ppositional defiant disorder (ODD) is a collection of chronic, negative, and hostile behaviors rather than a single coherent brain disorder, according to the U.S. Surgeon General's mental health report (U.S. Department of Health and Human Services, 1999). The *Diagnostic and*

Statistical Manual of Mental Disorders (American Psychiatric Association, 2000) definition goes on to add that these patterns of negativity and defiance persist for at least six months. ODD is characterized as a tendency to bother others and exhibit an argumentative and confrontational attitude, aggressiveness toward peers, and a disregard for how others feel. Individuals with ODD don't choose to act out in this manner. Underlying causes of the disorder are a combination of the child's temperament, biochemical components, environmental issues, and perceived neglect. The brain of a person with ODD essentially gets stuck, much like a scratched CD repeats the same note over and over. In addition, depression and tics manifest themselves in people with ODD.

A student with ODD has a social operating system that is not up to the demands of a school environment. Could this student flourish later in life if he or she continues to be oppositional? Absolutely! In fact, many who are oppositional find workplace situations where they are typically by themselves. Unfortunately, however, many end up in jobs around people and create toxic workplaces. For this reason, it is prudent to build their social skills. Fortunately, even in severe cases, the brain can change.

IMPACT

ODD is more than just kids behaving badly and should be taken seriously. This disorder rarely goes away; it requires interventions. ODD sufferers do not respond to reasonable persuasion, regardless of self-interest. Their opposition to all authority figures, especially parents and teachers, is pervasive and constant. Academic failure and poor social adjustment are common complications.

Timing is a key element in identifying an ODD sufferer. The behaviors must last at least six months for diagnosis, during which multiple (four or more) indicating behaviors are present and other possibilities should be ruled out (e.g., exposure to trauma).

Some improvement is possible when intervention occurs early. The more time that passes without treatment, however, the more entrenched and acute the disorder becomes. Physicians report that it is rare to see a patient with only ODD. It is usually accompanied by other neuropsychiatric conditions such as attention deficit disorder (ADD), anxiety, or depression.

Demographics

There has been a steady increase in symptoms of oppositional and defiant behaviors in school-age populations. Typical defiance or resistance should not be confused with ODD. For example, oppositional behaviors exhibited in 18- to 36-month-old children are part of a normal developmental phase. It is the persistence of severe and pervasive oppositional behaviors that signifies a problem.

Figure 3.1 Prevalence of ODD in America

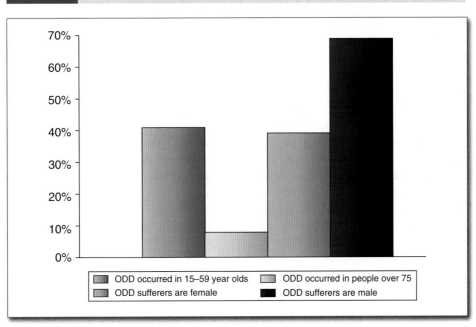

Source: U.S. Census Bureau, 2004.

Before puberty, ODD is more common in boys. After puberty, rates are nearly equal in boys and girls. ODD is found in one out of every five 3-year-old children (Lavigne et al., 2001). It is a disorder of childhood and adolescence that can begin informally as early as age 3 or 4, but usually begins by age 8. (Consult Figure 3.1 for more specifics on the prevalence of ODD in America.) In some children, it might become a conduct disorder or mood disorder.

ODD appears to run in families and is more likely to afflict children who have an alcoholic parent and/or a parent who has been in trouble with the law. The reason for this correlation may be that the troubled parent had ODD as a child and is now suffering from antisocial personality disorder. In other words, the correlation may be more genetic than environmental. There is some indication that ODD can develop into passive-aggressive personality disorder, anxiety disorder, or antisocial personality disorder in adulthood. There is also a correlation, although not causal, with obsessive-compulsive disorder. In many cases, however, reasonable social and occupational adjustment can be made with appropriate intervention and treatment.

Commentary

The base prevalence rates of ODD are estimated to be 6 to 10 percent in surveys of nonclinical, nonreferred samples of parents' reports (U.S. Department of Health and Human Services, 1999). ODD problems account for half or more of all mental health referrals.

ODD is characterized by the sufferer's annoyance with the behavior of others—which is perceived to be intentionally hurtful—and by aggressiveness rather than impulsiveness. Those with ODD often have difficulty stopping inappropriate behaviors. They become so used to being stuck in a behavior that it becomes more comfortable to fight change than to do what others want them to do. When others continually become annoyed with ODD sufferers, it is easier to develop a combative attitude.

ODD is difficult to live with in either the classroom or the home environment, and those diagnosed with but ODD and attention deficit hyperactivity disorder represent a huge challenge. The combined effect of impulsivity, hyperactivity, oppositional behavior, and defiance often leads to fights, rough play, and serious temper tantrums.

ODD constitutes a moderate to high level of challenge to the classroom teacher. You can contribute to success of learners with this disorder, but you will need support from others—notably parents and mental health professionals.

Likely Causes

The specific cause of ODD is unknown at this time, but the following theories have been proposed.

Temperament

Most experts think that inherent personality or temperament contributes to the disorder, and the effects may be heightened when parents aren't educated about the condition and don't seek professional help. Since ODD often coexists with other problems, such as ADD, anxiety, and depression, it is difficult to isolate the definitive causes.

In many cases a problem is evident almost from birth and becomes even more pronounced over time. These kids are simply more rigid and demanding. They have a heightened need to be in control right from the start.

Trauma Incidence

There is a higher incidence of childhood trauma among those with ODD. Exposure to head trauma, neglect, divorce, environmental toxins, or sexual and/or physical abuse may predispose one to ODD. Conversely, it should be noted that a traumatic childhood does not necessarily lead to social misbehavior.

Parental Alcoholism

There is some evidence that a correlation may exist between ODD and one or both parents being alcoholic.

Chemical Dysregulation

One cause (or symptom) may be a dysfunctional serotonin system. Typically, in patients with ODD, the cingulate gyrus (in the back of the frontal lobes) is hyperactive, with abnormally low levels of serotonin. Blood and saliva tests show that these patients have lower levels of serotonin, which is known to regulate cognitive flexibility.

Heredity

Researchers have been studying gene variants associated with the dopamine system and their potential relationship to disorders and behaviors that are comorbid (overlapping) with drug abuse. Some researchers have proposed that there is a genetic basis for a reward-deficiency syndrome consisting of addictive, impulsive, and compulsive behavior and personality disorders.

Neurological Disorders

Associations have been made between ODD symptoms and some neurological disorders such as epilepsy.

Brain Areas Involved

Behavioral differences typically correlate with brain differences. Brain scans show metabolic differences in an ODD brain versus a typical brain, and the areas involved include the cingulate gyrus, the amygdala, and the basal ganglia (see Figures 3.2 and 3.3). Increased activity in the left temporal lobe is also implicated in ODD and may contribute to irritability. Also, the prefrontal cortex functioning fails to inhibit impulsive, repetitive behaviors (Evans, Gonnella, Marcynyszyn, Gentile, & Salpekar, 2005).

Cingulate Gyrus

The cingulate gyrus, which runs longitudinally through the middle of the frontal lobes, serves as a "gear shifter" in the brain and allows us to move smoothly from one state to another (Clarke, Dalley, Crofts, Robbins, & Roberts, 2004; Kondo, Osaka, & Osaka, 2005). In patients with ODD, the cingulate gyrus is typically overactive (see Figures 3.2 and 3.3), which may intensify oppositional behaviors and make it biologically difficult for the sufferer to stop a thought at will and move on. But some medications and behavioral therapy approaches have shown promise in reducing the overactivity of this area.

Amygdala

Since ODD sufferers often have little, if any, fear of consequences, the amygdala (a small structure in the temporal lobes that regulates fear) has

| Figure 3.2 | A Healthy Brain Versus a Brain With ODD |

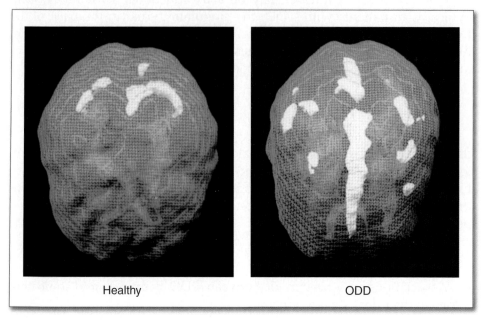

Healthy   ODD

Source: Images courtesy of Daniel Amen, MD.

also been implicated. Excess fearlessness has been correlated with limit-breaking and boundary-breaking behaviors later in life, whereas cautious, fearful behaviors are associated with a stronger conscience and cooperation.

Basal Ganglia

Though the relationship at this point is still tentative, there is some evidence that the basal ganglia, located in the lower midbrain area, may be linked to the thinking and acting out of oppositional and impulsive thoughts. The basal ganglia is also highly involved with making smooth transitions in thinking, moving, and managing anxiety.

Neurotransmitter Levels

Noadrenaline (also known as norepinephrine) is the neurotransmitter of arousal, high energy, and urgency. It influences us tremendously, especially during the fight-or-flight response. It is produced by the adrenal glands and helps maintain consistent blood pressure. It also regulates arousal moods and emotions. The locus ceruleus, which is in the midbrain, releases noradrenaline. While the baseline level of noradrenaline is typically just high enough to keep us motivated and to provide a reserve of energy, some individuals (including ODD sufferers) may produce an

Figure 3.3	Diagram of the Brain's Dysfunction in ODD Patients

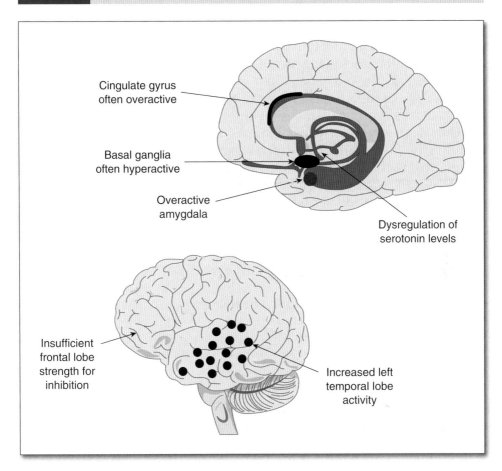

Cingulate gyrus often overactive

Basal ganglia often hyperactive

Overactive amygdala

Dysregulation of serotonin levels

Insufficient frontal lobe strength for inhibition

Increased left temporal lobe activity

unusually high level of noradrenaline. Under these circumstances, even a small stimulus will create unusually strong arousal. The individual may respond to little things with anxiety, fear, or overreactivity. Conversely, when an individual has an abnormally low level of noradrenaline, higher levels of stimulation are required to activate normal feelings of energy and aliveness.

Anatomical Anomalies

Anatomical anomalies are not prevalent or consistent in patients with ODD, so an MRI is of little value. In some cases, such as when an individual is involved in a serious accident, a PET (positron emission tomography) scan or SPECT (single positron emission computerized tomography) image, may help in identifying metabolic changes. However, there is no evidence that scanning by itself can provide an ODD diagnosis.

Recognizable Symptoms

ODD involves a pattern of defiant, angry, antagonistic, hostile, irritable, and/or vindictive behaviors; however, it does not necessarily involve violent offenses. Sufferers typically blame others for their problems. They can be frustrating, tricky, aggressive, and deceitful, but in general they are not dangerous. While most children will comply with an adult's reasonable requests about 7 times out of 10, children with ODD will generally comply 3 or fewer times—and sometimes never.

The simple questions to ask yourself are: How often does the student comply with my requests? Does the behavior occur more frequently than is typically observed in individuals of comparable age and developmental level? Consider the following diagnostic criteria, along with frequency of behaviors and duration period:

- losing one's temper
- arguing with adults
- defying adults or refusing adults' requests or rules
- deliberately annoying others
- blaming others for one's own mistakes or misbehavior
- being touchy or easily annoyed
- being angry and resentful
- being spiteful or vindictive for no apparent reason
- swearing or using obscene language
- holding a low opinion of oneself

Diagnosing ODD is not without its challenges. It is complicated by high rates of comorbidity with attention deficit hyperactivity disorder as well as abuse, attachment disorders, neglect, and head injury. For an accurate diagnosis, it is important to understand that ODD behavior occurs more frequently than is typically observed in individuals of comparable age and developmental level; causes clinically significant impairment in social, academic, or occupational functioning; and occurs outside of any other diagnosis.

WHAT YOU CAN DO

Although dealing with ODD is challenging for everyone involved, you can contribute to the success of learners who suffer from this disorder. ODD is not acute, so there's no need to go into emergency mode. By taking a calm and steady approach to the problem, you will help reduce ODD sufferers' stress as well as your own.

First, their social operating system is clearly not up to the task of the school's social environment, so it will have to be strengthened. (Strategies for doing so are discussed in Chapter 2 and in the next section of this chapter.) Do not get sidetracked in pursuing your plan. Here are the essentials:

1. Believe that it will work; know that the brain can and will change with appropriate interventions.

2. Build a team, and make a plan so that every person is on the same page.

3. Focus on building the operating system.

4. Always maintain relationships throughout the process.

5. Be positive and patient. This will take time.

The strategies described in the following section can help turn what might at first feel like a hopeless situation into a constructive situation.

Seek Support/Create a Response Team

You will need the support of others, notably school administrators, other teachers, the child's parents, a medical doctor, and mental health professionals. Once you've identified the key support team members, get them together to talk face to face outside of the student's presence. Consistent communication between the child's parents, between school and home, and between medical/treatment professionals and other concerned parties is crucial. This team approach can help offset the child's tendency to play one person or group off another. All of the child's care-givers (e.g., grandparents, relatives, babysitters) need to understand ODD and the treatment plan.

Develop a Plan

With the help of a therapist and a physician, develop an intervention plan. Also discuss strategies for dealing with the oppositional and defiant behavior. If you react on the spur of the moment, your emotions will guide you wrongly in dealing with students with ODD. They try to provoke intense feelings in everyone. A written and agreed-upon plan should outline exactly what response is appropriate for each pattern of behavior. For example, what should be done if a child disrupts class, annoys others, gets in a fight, throws a major temper tantrum, makes suicidal threats, or declares that he or she is going to run away? Whatever the response, all parties involved with the child must adhere to the plan. See that all parties are on board and agree to not buy into the oppositional behavior exhibited by the child.

Use a Behavior-Modification Approach

A behavior-modification approach can help manage the child with ODD both at home and at school. However, rewards and punishments should be mutually agreed upon and considered in light of the child's specific temperament and personal issues. In other words, a formula approach does not work with children with ODD. The rewards should not be money or material things, but rather privileges or activities that you know the child enjoys. Use a mix of negative and positive reinforcers. A typical positive reinforcer, for example, might be a later bedtime on the weekend or the opportunity to choose the dinner menu for the evening. A typical negative reinforcer might be revoking of TV privileges.

Respond in a Nonoppositional Way

Inflexible teachers or caretakers who react with intense emotions will fail in dealing effectively with the behavior of a child with ODD. If a student stomps his or her feet and says, "You can't make me!," it's better to agree with the student and instead use reverse psychology. Try saying, "You're right, I can't make you. Nobody can, not even you. Yeah, that's right. I don't even think you can make yourself do it!" Over and over teachers will be challenged, and over and over they must learn to take a deep breath, relax, and avoid confrontation. Seek common ground, and if it's not there, create it. If the student stomps out of the room, for example, call a break and then initiate a quick state-change activity, such as outdoor story time, a group skip around the playground, or a new game. This strategy won't work every time, but it's important to understand that when adults respond with an oppositional approach, the problem worsens and can easily turn into a full-scale war.

As mentioned earlier in the chapter, when an ODD sufferer's brain gets stuck, don't take the resulting lack of change personally. The sufferer does not make rapid changes easily and is more likely to change his or her state when the chosen subject is his or her idea, when he or she is given advance warning to warm up to an idea, and when change does not require issues of power, authority, or obedience.

Confirm Stories

Usually, students with ODD do not regard themselves as the problem, but rather blame others. Some try to convince adults that their parents have mistreated them; others try to convince parents that their teachers are treating them unfairly. Obviously, this can keep everyone off balance and delay or prevent proper intervention, so it is important to confirm with others the reality of the situation.

Be Consistent

Do not bend the rules with students with ODD. It is very important to remain consistent both individually and across caretaker lines. For example, if a child is not allowed to eat candy at home, grandparents, babysitters, and teachers need to follow this rule as well. A firm, authoritative style does not have to be in conflict with a loving, affectionate approach. The key is to be consistent in your expectations and to voice them in a kind and loving way. Consequences for breaking the rules should be fairly and dispassionately administered. Share the treatment/behavior modification plan with all involved parties so that discipline responses remain consistent.

Isolate and Prioritize Behavior Issues

Prioritize the behaviors you wish to address first; then focus your responses on the targeted behaviors. Rather than trying to teach the child to "be good," you might try, for example, to encourage the child not to pout or swear.

Be Specific With Your Requests

When you request something from a child with ODD, you must be very clear and specific (see Table 3.1). For example, rather than saying, "Listen when I tell you something," it would be better to say, "Please sit down and look at me when I ask you to listen." If the ODD sufferer can read, create a list of simple, straightforward ground rules (or expectations) that you can make into a poster for the home and/or classroom. Consider the appropriateness of asking the student to sign a contract agreeing to the ground rules.

Table 3.1   Classroom Dos and Don'ts for Learners With ODD

Dos	Don'ts
Provide encouragement, just as you would with any other student.	Get caught up in arguing with ODD sufferers—you'll always lose. Even if you win, you lose when the relationship suffers.
Use a lot of writing, journaling, and drawing. These activities are great for encouraging positive and appropriate expression. They also help ODD sufferers sort out their thoughts and feelings. Focus on the process, rather than the product.	Be adamant in your approach or expectations.
Let go of tight control; try to be flexible.	Give ultimatums.
Give choices. Use double binds in which both ways will work.	Become obsessed by students with ODD. Work instead for slow and steady progress.
Try to remember that an unhealthy brain causes kids (and adults) to act in unproductive ways (like resisting everything).	Overlook their inappropriate behaviors, add fuel to the fire, or lock into tug-of-war with ODD sufferers.

REVISITING THE STUDENT

Remember "Miguel," one of the learners introduced in the pretest at the front of the book? He's also the student who fits the profile for ODD. Like the others, Miguel is unique—he exhibits a pattern of symptoms that are associated with a specific disorder. However, some of these symptoms can be observed in other conditions as well. This is why you want to look for patterns, rather than isolated behaviors. To help you remember what's important in assessing students with ODD, take a moment, relax, and focus on the photo, the symptoms, and the key points of this chapter.

Symptoms

- Often loses temper; is angry, spiteful, vindictive, and resentful
- Argues with adults; defies authority and rejects adults' requests or rules; complies about 10 to 20 percent of the time
- Deliberately annoys others and is easily annoyed
- Blames others for his or her own mistakes or misbehavior
- Is angry and resentful; is vindictive for no apparent reason
- Swears and uses obscene language

SUPPLEMENTAL RESOURCES

Books

Antisocial Behavior in School: Strategies and Best Practices, by Geoffrey Colvin

Brain Lock, by Jeffrey Schwartz

Change Your Brain, Change Your Life, by Daniel G. Amen, MD

Ghosts From the Nursery, by Robin Karr-Morse and Meredith Wiley

If My Kid's So Nice . . . Why Is He Driving Me Crazy? by James Sutton

Web sites

American Academy of Child and Adolescent Psychiatry: www.aacap.org

Mayo Clinic: www.mayoclinic.com

National Institute on Drug Abuse: www.nida.nih.gov

National Institutes of Health: www.nih.gov

Plato Learning: www.studyweb.com

Dr. James Sutton: www.docspeak.com

4

The Resigned Learner

Learned Helplessness

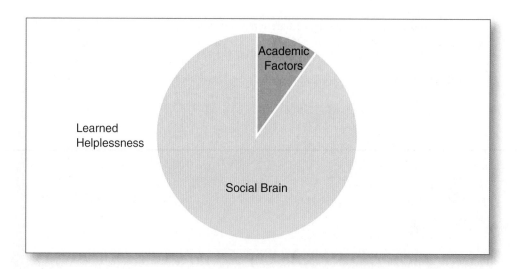

We have all seen students who have simply given up. They sit in class disconnected, almost zombie-like in their demeanor. While it's easy to call them lazy, there's often more to it than that. Not every student who is disconnected has a behavior disorder. In fact, most of them simply need more relevant and challenging curriculum delivered in a more engaging, brain-friendly way by a passionate, responsive, caring teacher. But when that dose of good instruction is not working, usually there's a different problem.

When there is a failure to avoid or escape an unpleasant or aversive stimulus that occurs as a result of previous exposure to unavoidable painful stimuli, it is referred to as learned helplessness (LH). LH is a behavioral condition (not a "disorder" in the *Diagnostic and Statistical Manual of Mental Disorders* [American Psychiatric Association, 2000]) that is characterized by apathy, lack of motivation, and helplessness in the face of normal, everyday problems and challenges. It is characterized by questions such as these: "Why bother?" "What's the point?" "Who cares?"

LH is the result of feeling chronically powerless over a situation or believing a negative outcome will occur independent of one's response. Individuals with LH believe that no matter what they do, they can't succeed; thus, a pattern of passivity and withdrawal occurs, and the recognition that potential solutions exist is totally lost. Once acute helplessness is experienced in an area of their life, transference to other areas is common. This expectation of failure, if not reversed, eventually interferes with learning, achievement, and, ultimately, success in life.

Just a generation ago, students suffering from this condition were mislabeled "lazy." Fortunately, today we know better. LH is not genetic. It is learned. And therefore, the good news is that it can be unlearned! But do not make the mistake of assuming a child can willfully control the situation. The root of the problem, in fact, is lack of control.

In animal studies, subjects exposed to chronic failure and negative outcomes eventually exhibit symptoms similar to depressed subjects. They become sedentary, unwilling to even try to succeed, and disinterested in experiencing pleasure (anhedonia). They may cease to groom, eat, or have sex and may exhibit self-destructive behaviors.

In humans, when LH reaches this state of seriousness, learning is, of course, impaired. Even providing tangible rewards to modify the behavior is pointless at this stage because the subjects have stopped paying attention. In human studies, unsolvable tasks induce mild LH quite easily, and providing tangible rewards actually induces greater helplessness. The typical cycle, as shown in Figure 4.1, shows the key factors involved in either LH or responsiveness.

Although the condition is easily transferred from one life situation to another, it can also exist in a singular context. For example, a student may perform well in all classes except math. In a case like this, the student probably experienced repeated failure or a feeling of powerlessness in the subject early on. Subsequently, associations with the subject may trigger an episode of LH. Some teachers accidentally trigger LH by giving students overly challenging tasks without the appropriate support and/or resources. Testing situations can also trigger LH symptoms. The determining factor here is perceived control over desirable outcomes.

Figure 4.1   Cycle in Learned Helplessness or Responsiveness

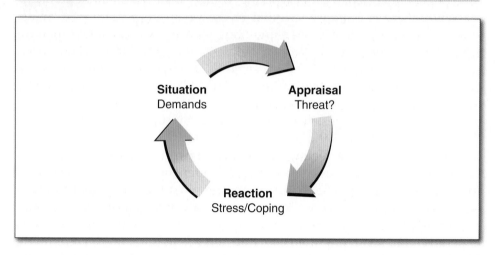

IMPACT

In the best-case scenario, LH will be unlearned (with the help of a vigilant teacher and parents) before it digs its ugly teeth in for the long haul. Without effective intervention, unfortunately LH sufferers run the risk of sinking into the vicious cycle of failure that, in the worst-case scenario, can result in a long-term disorder such as depression. Fortunately, however, this is a condition that can be reversed. Your challenge as the teacher is to ensure that children with LH experience many consistent successes. Once their feelings of accomplishment outweigh their feelings of failure, they will be on the road to recovery.

If LH students' needs are ignored, you run the risk that they will commonly disrupt the entire class. Negative behavior patterns can be an unconscious plea for help or a means of disguising the inadequacy that students with LH feel. Although no special measures in particular need to be taken, sound teaching practices are paramount when dealing with the sensitivities of these learners. Although medication and behavioral therapy are sometimes indicated in the treatment of LH, this is definitely a condition that you can treat in the classroom.

Demographics

Most of us, at some point in our lives, are at risk for developing LH depending on our previous exposure to success or failure, empowerment, or impotency. A high incidence occurs in people with epilepsy, displaced populations, and individuals suffering from depression. Because there is far more relevancy and hands-on learning at the elementary level, incidence of LH is significantly higher in junior and senior high school students when compared to elementary students.

Females exhibit a higher incidence of LH compared to males. And LH among white and black high school females has been shown to be positively associated with weight-related psychological conditions. In animal subjects, interestingly enough, it is the most rather than least aggressive who are most at risk for LH.

Commentary

LH develops most commonly as a result of overwhelming or pernicious sensory input, which we cannot control, typically in the form of exposure to either serious or repeated trauma with accompanying fear or helplessness. LH is different from temporary apathy or lack of motivation—characteristics that are not uncommon in school-age learners. Many reasons exist for apathy, so don't automatically assume without sufficient observation that a child has LH. It is important to rule out temporary situational causes. Only symptoms that are chronic and persistent are indicative of LH, and even then a more serious disorder, such as depression, may ultimately be the diagnosis. The following examples illustrate how LH can be confused with other conditions:

- Apathy and inactivity are also evident among individuals suffering from depression.
- A teacher-student conflict or mismatch in learning and teaching styles can elicit symptoms similar to those of LH.
- The use of irrelevant or inappropriate curriculum can cause apathy.
- Apathy is a typical response to drug abuse, malnutrition, and/or trauma.
- Negative associations related to a previous failure may also trigger apathy.
- Fatigue and/or sleep disorders affect motivation levels.

Although LH shares significant symptom overlap with depression, there is an identifiable distinction. LH sufferers stop trying to cope with their perceived loss of control ("I can't change the circumstances, so why try?"). People with depression, on the other hand, internalize past failures to the point that their thinking becomes distorted and global ("Nothing I do works, and everything sucks anyway.").

Individuals who are comfortable with risk and failure and who have somehow learned to maintain a positive attitude when faced with adversity are less likely to succumb to LH. For example, when student A fails a math exam, he extrapolates that he didn't study hard enough, whereas student B extrapolates that she's "stupid." Student B has personalized and globalized the failure and attributed it to an internal mechanism (e.g., IQ), which she has no control over, versus an external mechanism (e.g., amount of study time), which she could certainly control.

Other comments that students with LH typically make include the following: "I'm just not good at math," "I was unlucky; it was Friday the 13th," "I don't get along with the teachers," "The system is fixed," "I'm never alert at test time," "The tests are always hard," "I never have time to study," and "There are always students who beat the curve." Each of these perceived causes can be categorized in three ways:

- internal vs. external (a personal trait vs. an environmental or circumstantial situation)
- specific vs. universal ("Mr. Jones talks too fast for me to understand what he means." vs. "Math is just too hard for me.")
- temporary vs. permanent ("I didn't do as well as I would have liked to on the test." vs. "I'll never pass math.")

The most pessimistic explanatory style is correlated with the greatest likelihood of LH. For example, the statement "I'm stupid" is internal (or personal), universal, and permanent. It conveys a sense of discouragement, hopelessness, and despair. A more optimistic person would blame someone or something external. For example, he or she might say, "The teacher gave an especially hard test this time." The most optimistic explanatory style is external, specific, and temporary ("I didn't do as well as I know I could have if I had studied more.").

Conversely, in response to a positive event, students with LH might explain their success as something out of their control. For example, when achieving a high score on a math exam, a student might say, "I was lucky that day," discounting his or her intelligence. The optimist, on the other hand, would attribute the success to something more personal by saying something such as "I'm so smart." We often learn explanatory styles from our parents. These styles are important because they shape our beliefs, which drive our actions, which impact our success in life.

The consistent theme here is *control*. When learners perceive that they have no control over troubling experiences, LH is likely to develop. But when students learn that they do, in fact, have control over their thoughts and actions, they become proactive, persistent, resourceful, and, ultimately, immune to LH. Thus, you can contribute immensely to the prevention and reversal of LH by empowering students more and controlling them less.

Likely Causes

The risk of LH varies significantly among people since perception plays a key role. The nature of the condition is exposure to an adverse environmental event combined with a parallel lack of coping skills. This suggests that the strongest likelihood is that genes are less predictive than environmental factors.

Neglect/Negative Role Modeling

Neglect of any kind, especially during the first few years of life, creates fertile ground for LH to take hold. Beyond this, if caretakers who feel helpless surround a child, the risk of that child becoming helpless is much higher (as is sometimes reflected in families who have been on welfare for more than a generation). Therefore, some would say LH is "contagious."

Trauma-Induced Debilitation

It is possible for LH to be induced by a traumatic experience when all three of the following conditions are present: intense negative experience, a perceived lack of control during the trauma, and the sufferer deciding at some point to stop trying and thus forming a paralyzing belief. Paralyzing beliefs can be categorized as follows:

- internal ("The problem is me.")
- universal ("It happens in all areas of my life.")
- permanent ("It will always happen, so why try?")

Unconscious Enabling

Teachers (or parents) who do too much for students can, over time, inadvertently reinforce or even induce helplessness. For example, a teacher who repeatedly brings a sharpened pencil to a student's desk instead of having the student get up to sharpen it him- or herself can unconsciously fuel the child's sense of helplessness. The teacher's intentions may be benign, but over time the child may begin to question his or her own competency. Children need to be taught how to take care of themselves and that struggle and mistakes are a natural part of the learning process. Well-meaning parents may think they are saving their child from failure by doing, rather than helping with, the child's homework, but the result of this kind of help is a removal of the natural consequences and feedback necessary for growth. When children are overly guarded from failure, they develop an intense fear of it.

Internalized/Externalized Oppression

LH tends to take hold in individuals who mistakenly attribute their failures to a character defect (e.g., "I'm just stupid."). Along this line of thinking, children who overhear a teacher or parent say they are lazy, incapable, or lagging behind their classmates in a particular subject may internalize the comment to the degree that it becomes a self-fulfilling prophecy. Some LH sufferers, on the other hand, experience the opposite distortion: they blame their failures on others, the "bad" school, or the world as a whole. As a result, they have given up any sense of control.

This tendency toward distorted thinking may, ultimately, be what determines an individual's susceptibility to LH. The circular path from our thoughts to our behaviors is pretty clear cut. Our experiences shape our expectations and explanations, which shape our beliefs and reinforce our mental states, which in turn regulate our feelings of worthiness, competence, and potency, and ultimately impact our actions and responses to the world. Once a distortion takes hold, we inadvertently reinforce our original experience until the cycle is broken.

Students with LH are low-frequency responders, which means that some students have been unresponsive for so long that they actually forget what it feels like to be engaged. It can even feel uncomfortable to be responsive. It's best to respect their condition, but still avoid giving up on them. The longer someone spends time in any metabolic state (e.g., anger, sleep, optimism), the more committed the nervous system becomes to maintaining that state. In time, it may become the default state. This means it can become more comfortable to revert to that state than a so-called better state. The implications of this situation are profound.

With counterproductive default states, students feel powerless. Students want to feel more confident and more capable, but most of them simply don't know how to do this purposely. As the teacher, you can empower students to manage their own states.

Brain Areas Involved

All behaviors are dependent on the state that one is in. The path to engagement is through reading and managing the states. The longer anyone is in any state, the more stable he or she becomes. The brain is the integral gatekeeper to the behavior response system.

Genes

Research suggests a genetic susceptibility to LH, but it is highly interactive with environmental influences (Stein & Stein, 2008). Animal models also suggest that mRNA expression is affected by induced acute stress (Sands, Strong, Corbitt, & Morilak, 2000), and stress responses suggest a genetic link (King, Abend, & Edwards, 2001). Overall, these studies suggest a potential genetic link of susceptibility to anxiety and stress disorders.

Frontal Lobes

Decisions are made in the medial-frontal cortex. In humans, multiple brain areas are involved in LH, but they do not create the disorder; rather, they are always present at the "scene of the crime." While the biological substrates evident in LH may influence the condition, it is the perceived absence of control, a psychological factor, that is key to its development. However, the variable of control does have significant biological consequences.

Neurotransmitter Levels

Evidence suggests that chronic depletion of norepinephrine is evident in LH sufferers. Produced in the locus ceruleus at the top of the brainstem and spreading to all areas of the brain, this neurotransmitter influences mood, arousal, and memory. LH sufferers have also been found to have chronic depletions of gamma aminobutyric acid (GABA) and serotonin (a mood regulator) and elevated analgesic (opiate) levels.

Hypothalamus

After a stressful episode, the hypothalamus releases corticotropin-releasing factor (CRF). When CRF reaches the pituitary gland it begins a chemical cascade in the body that eventually results in the release of cortisol from the adrenals.

Recognizable Symptoms

Because LH can be easily confused with other conditions, it is important to pay close attention. Observe the student over a period of time and, if possible, record what you see in a notebook or journal. The symptoms common to LH include the following:

- apathy and inertia
- diminished response initiation (unresponsive to shocking events)
- perceived lack of control over environment and circumstances
- lack of assertiveness
- lack of hostility when it is warranted
- lack of motivation
- increased sarcasm
- statements of powerlessness ("What's the point?" "Why bother?" "Who cares?" "So what?")
- automaton-like behaviors (going through the motions)
- cognition problems
- loss of appetite and weight
- lethargy
- unwillingness to socialize

WHAT YOU CAN DO

Fortunately, the effects of LH typically diminish over time as they are aided by the normal day-to-day circumstances, responsibilities, emergencies, and developmental stages of life. Nevertheless, it is important to intervene on a student's behalf with effective classroom strategies as soon as you notice the symptoms of LH.

Remember, an LH sufferer's social operating system (see pie chart at the beginning of this chapter) is clearly not up to the task of the school's social environment, so it will have to be strengthened. (Strategies for doing so are discussed in Chapter 2 and in the next section of this chapter.) Do not get sidetracked in pursuing your plan. Here are the essentials:

1. Believe that it will work. Know that the brain can and will change with appropriate interventions.

2. Build a team, and make a plan so that every person is on the same page.

3. Focus on building the operating system. In this case, focus on managing states and developing the student's ability to evaluate potential rewards (although not physical rewards) by taking action.

4. Always maintain relationships throughout the process.

5. Be positive and patient. This will take time.

If you suspect the more serious disorder, depression (which shares some LH symptoms), the student needs, at the very least, to be referred to the school psychologist immediately. In both conditions, the student may be passive, unwilling to participate, and feeling down, but in the case of depression, his or her perception of the disorder is personal ("I'm the problem, and I'm no good. So things will turn out badly."). Conversely, the student with LH perceives the problem as circumstantial ("Whatever I do, I can't change the situation, so it doesn't matter. I can't change anything, so why try?").

Due to the serious implications of depression (e.g., risk of suicide), individuals with depression should receive professional therapeutic treatment without delay. Students with LH, however, can usually be aided by a competent teacher and sensitive parents without therapeutic intervention. With a good solid program that ensures small steps toward success, LH can be alleviated within a few weeks or months.

It is not uncommon for parents to blame LH on the school or teachers. This line of thinking clearly stalls progress and can be extremely frustrating for conscientious teachers who understand the deeper implications of the condition. LH can be the result of a single traumatic incident, or it can develop over time. Certainly, institutions that inadvertently condition students to fail contribute to its incidence. This speaks to the importance of hiring effective teachers and administrators who reinforce optimistic thinking and appropriate learner control. Administrators who empower their teachers ultimately empower their students.

It is essential to create a highly engaging atmosphere where students are encouraged to stay active, relate to others, and reflect on their learning. It may take some time to rewire the brain of a student suffering from LH, so don't get discouraged. LH didn't set in overnight, and it's not going to completely go away overnight. However, with a consistent approach that ensures multiple small successes throughout the learning unit, the student with LH will begin to show substantial progress. Above all else, never give up hope on reaching this student, because as soon as you give up, he or she will, too.

Engage Positive States

Students' behaviors tend to be consistent with their most common metabolic state. To change the behavior, first you must change the state. States provide a pool of choices from which all behaviors emerge. One pool contains only our silly, wild, crazy behaviors. A different pool contains our more serious, intellectual, thoughtful behaviors. Students with LH behave the way they do partly because their nervous system is conditioned by spending large amounts of waking hours in that state.

This speaks to the virtue of frequent classroom changes in states. Over time, such changes can alter learners' default state and reduce rigidity. When most students get frequent state changes, they are happy with the novelty. An LH sufferer's default (helpless) state can become self-reinforcing if the student spends extended time in it. More states elicit greater learner flexibility and far fewer instances of being stuck in a state.

Your classroom goal should be to create micro state changes that constantly engage students in the intellectual pool. The more often you keep students engaged, the easier it is to hold their attention and the less prone they are to become lethargic. Some strategies of engagement include providing the following instructions: "Take in a slow, deep breath . . . hold it . . . and now slowly . . . let it out," "Please angle your chair to face others so now you've got a group of four," and "Let's vote: how many of you think No. 1 is the most plausible? Raise your hand." The key is to continually involve students.

Martin Seligman's book *Learned Optimism* discusses a well-tested positive psychotherapy process in three key parts: positive states, an engaged life, and a meaningful life (Seligman, 1998). In the positive states phase, outline the past, present, and future. The past is used as a reflective period to focus on joys, successes, friendships, pride, and fulfillment of each student's afternoon. During an evaluation of the present, focus on savoring the moment and completing one savoring activity, retelling a neighbor what happened, or sharing a story in class while standing at the front of the room. To create a sense of hope and optimism, instill a forward-looking outlook for events to create positive change.

If you find a student in a negative default state, do not blame the student—it is likely an adaptive response to an adverse situation (perhaps serious problems at home) and a chronic conditioned response that will not go away immediately. Be a stable force who is in it for the long haul.

Relationships grow with consistency, building on small gains, which over time lead to success.

Be Enthusiastic

Part of the solution is your own enthusiasm, consistency of strategy, and belief in success. The other part is empowering students so that they take on a greater class role, including doing the following tasks:

- taking care of the class music
- providing leadership and making announcements
- submitting test questions
- doing class chores
- leading energizers and stretching
- participating in student juries for discipline

To empower slow responders, you have to continue to build the relationship; without it, you have little to go on. Find out their areas of interest and expertise—this should get them excited. Then give them jobs with responsibilities. Empowering students means teaching them how to manage their own states. Suggestions you can make about activities to do outside of class include the following:

- cycle, walk, swim
- learning about better nutrition
- naps/sleep
- service work
- pleasure reading
- busy work/chores

Provide Enrichment

Never underestimate the power of enrichment to establish changes in the brain. Your response is important in terms of the momentum of students' success, literally and figuratively. All the body's cells respond to either conservation or growth strategies. But inconsistent programs and efforts equate mixed messages and no progress. Enrichment strategies influence the body from micro levels (single cells and individual neurons) to macro levels (brain and body systems).

Continue to challenge students in order to create meaningful learning. Intense comprehension programs that strengthen life skills over a week or more include Outward Bound and SuperCamp. These are quick and effective, as are martial arts and dance classes. If traveling and camping are not feasible options, then consider physical education. Provide opportunities for voluntary, gross-motor repetitive activities, such as bicycling, swimming, power walking, and aerobics, four to six days a week.

REVISITING THE STUDENT

"Tom," one of the learners introduced in the pretest at the front of the book, is the student who fits the profile for LH. Like the others, Tom is unique—he exhibits a pattern of symptoms that are associated with a specific condition. However, some of these symptoms can be observed in other conditions or disorders as well. This is why you want to look for patterns, rather than isolated behaviors. To help you remember what's important in assessing students with LH, take a moment, relax, and focus on the photo, the symptoms, and the key points of this chapter.

Remember that timing is essential. Be in the realm of seeking and providing solutions for the long haul by never giving up on students. Accept that change comes in the tiniest of ways, usually taken one small step at a time. LH is a learned behavior; therefore, you can change it with new learning. While change unfolds internally for students, it may take months for you to see the progress by their repeated behaviors.

Symptoms

- Displays a high level of apathy, listlessness, or lack of vigor
- Passive and unresponsive in spite of shocking or surprising events
- Does not initiate new activities or learning
- Does not feel in control of his environment; likely to say, "What's the point?" "Why bother?" "Who cares?" or "So what?"
- Lack of hostility even when hostility is warranted
- Increased sarcasm

SUPPLEMENTAL RESOURCES

Books

Human Learned Helplessness, by Mario Mikulincer

Learned Helplessness and School Failure, by Robert and Myrna Gordon

Learned Helplessness: A Theory for the Age of Personal Control,
by Christopher Peterson, Steven F. Maier, and Martin E. P. Seligman

Learned Optimism, by Martin E. P. Seligman

Web sites

Learning Disabilities Association of California: www.ldaca.org

Outward Bound: www.outwardbound.org

SuperCamp: www.supercamp.com

5

The Out-of-Control Learner

Conduct Disorder

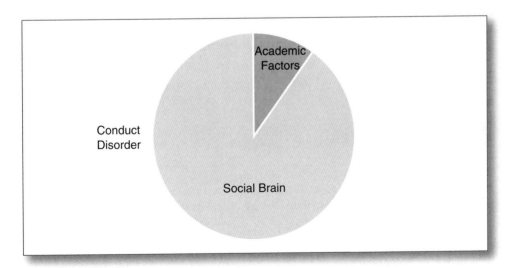

We've all seen kids get upset at school and get in fights. Of the thousands of fights that happen every month, some kids are getting involved for the first and only time in their life. Other kids have a recurring pattern of violence. These are the students with conduct disorder (CD), a severe, chronic, pathologically driven antisocial behavior. It is repetitive and persistent, and it infringes on the basic rights of others and/or violates major societal norms. Students with CD are not the occasional problem learners who disrupt class. Rather, they represent an acute and persistent challenge for teachers. CD can cause significant social, academic, and behavior problems. It is often highly stressful, pushing teachers and caregivers to the brink.

CD is highly correlated with violence and attention deficit disorder (ADD), which is why many times there is more than one disorder present. For example, there are some parallels between oppositional defiant disorder (ODD; see Chapter 3) and CD. However, the single biggest difference between the two is that students with CD will often hurt people, animals, and property with zero regard for safety or rules. Students with ODD will not cross these lines. CD symptoms are sometimes confused with those of other disorders, so ask yourself whether your learner is more like Student A or Student B described in Table 5.1.

As you may have guessed, Student A is likely seeking attention and/or needs an environmental change. He or she may be acting out in response to an inadequate situation (e.g., an inactive, stale learning environment; too little structure; poor nutrition; poor physical health; inconsistent rules and regulations). Student B represents a learner who may have CD. This student clearly needs to be dealt with in a serious fashion. Not only is it important to reduce the disruption to other students, but the sanity of the teacher and everyone's safety needs to be considered as well.

The good news is that CD is treatable over time. It is best if intervention starts early, around kindergarten to second grade.

Table 5.1 Which Student Has a Conduct Disorder?

Student A	Student B
• Exhibits excessive movement, loud talking, poor classroom manners, weak social skills, and poor posture • Teases particular classmates, fails to turn in homework or follow directions, talks out of turn, plays practical jokes, and often dominates classroom agendas	• Exhibits inappropriate emotional outbursts, an unwillingness to follow directions or cooperate with others, consistent verbal abuse, and a tendency to swat or hit classmates • Challenges authority, uses vulgar language, and intimidates others regularly; class disruptions, taunting, rudeness, and random acts of destruction are common

IMPACT

Chronic physical fighting at the preschool level may indicate severe problems later. If the fighting continues into middle school, there is a chance that the student will commit a violent crime. While any behavior problem creates challenges for teachers and other students, CD stretches the patience of all educators.

Demographics

CD is fortunately not as prevalent as some other less serious disorders, but it still poses a serious problem in the classroom. As you might guess, there is a far higher incidence of the disorder in males than females. Female behavior disorders are sometimes more difficult to diagnose. Research has shown that CD has both genetic and environmental components. A large percentage of children with CD have a parent who had a disruptive behavior disorder as a youngster. Children with CD often have an onset of it before the age of 10. It can begin as early as age 3 or 4, but usually is not diagnosed until students begin school. These kids generally go on to have a more difficult time in their academic performance and sociable relationships than their peers.

Commentary

Some may wonder what factors influence a rise of CD. The answer is multifaceted, but the culprits may include less family time, less structure at home, lack of a positive father figure, and large-scale social tolerance of violence. Children with disruptive behavior disorders such as CD have a very difficult time getting along in school. When compared to others, they usually have the worst academic performance records, the poorest relationships, and the weakest self-management skills (e.g., taking responsibility, planning, controlling anger, being punctual).

The issue of safety—a fine thread that distinguishes CD from other behavior problems (including ODD)—is another concern. Students suffering from CD tend to raise personal safety concerns for teachers, other students, family members, and/or themselves.

Although CD is very challenging, you can contribute to the success of children who suffer from it. You will, however, need a great deal of support from others, notably the children's parents, mental health professionals, and your school administration.

Likely Causes

Some might wonder what is going on in society that has increased the incidence of CD. There are many hypotheses, including an increase in violence and stressors, more sedentary lifestyle, poor nutrition, overcrowded schools, and greater acceptance of "in your face" talk. It is not known for sure what causes CD, but the following is a list of probable contributing factors.

Chemical Dysregulation

One cause (or symptom) of CD may be chronically low levels of cortisol and/or related neurotransmitters. Cortisol is secreted in response to stressful or threatening situations. Low levels may influence how young males respond to potential stressors. Boys with consistently lower cortisol levels seem to be unafraid of retribution. It is possible that since they don't feel stress in the same way, they don't develop the typical coping strategies, like avoidance.

Reduced Prefrontal Activity

Individuals with CD may have experienced abnormal neurological development before or after birth. The differences in brain activity cannot be explained by other factors, such as age, gender, ethnicity, handedness, schizophrenia, or generalized brain dysfunction. Another theory is that delivery complications at birth may cause neurological vulnerabilities (or brain insults) that contribute to the problem. Some evidence indicates that CD, in addition to a combination of ODD with ADD or a mood disorder, arises from similar cortical-subcortical loops.

Abuse/Family Environment

Sexual or physical abuse from a father does not by itself cause CD, but it is commonly found in cases of violent kids. Parents who are physically abusive and/or highly critical and hostile are more likely to have poorly adjusted children who exhibit behavior problems at school and home. These children also have more trouble establishing good relationships with their peers, teachers, and family members. When parents abuse drugs or suffer from depression, they are less responsive to their children's needs. The first 18 months of a child's life are particularly critical to the attachment and attunement process.

Children learn behavior by modeling. Students with CD may not come from homes where manners are preached and practiced. Children who consistently receive negative responses to social and emotional encounters with their primary caregiver(s) learn that people cannot be relied on, and they ultimately disconnect. In an abusive environment, they learn that the way to get their needs met is to be aggressive and/or violent.

Maltreatment (especially of girls) represents a significant risk factor for numerous other subsequent psychiatric conditions and behaviors beyond CD, including borderline personality disorder, antisocial personality disorder, posttraumatic stress disorder (syndrome), eating disorders, dissociative disorders, substance abuse, somatization disorder, suicide, depression, and self-mutilation.

Trauma

Early loss experiences may alter brain function in a way that renders children more susceptible to subsequent environmental stressors. In persons genetically predisposed to a disorder such as major depression, this could be a crucial factor in bringing any such predisposition to the fore.

Parental Substance Abuse

Abnormal fetal development due to maternal substance abuse and/or smoking during or before pregnancy may lead to subtle damaging effects on brain regions that control attention and movement.

Poor Parenting Skills

You may be wondering whether parenting strategies can contribute to the emergence of CD in children. When the parenting skills are low-average to good, the answer is no. Most cases of severe behavior disorders require at least one of the big three (abuse, residential instability, head injury) in addition to very poor parenting skills. Children with CD usually have two or more "strikes" against them. Adding any other variables adds fuel to the fire. Smaller factors (e.g., poor nutrition, drug abuse, negative peer groups) can exacerbate or accelerate the condition but by themselves are rarely causative.

Brain Areas Involved

Frontal Lobes

This area of the brain (including the medial prefrontal cortex to a moderate degree and the right orbitofrontal cortex to a more significant degree) is highly involved with inhibition and impulsiveness.

Midbrain

This area of the brain (including the hypothalamus all the way to the adrenals) is highly involved in the secretion of cortisol, which, as discussed earlier, is secreted in response to stressful or threatening situations.

Amygdala

This area of the brain is responsible for intense emotions such as rage. In students with CD, it may be hypersensitive to threat and distress, evoking more reactive impulses.

Genes

A strong genetic component is indicated. While someone may not necessarily be born with CD, he or she may be born with a temperament and chemistry that favors the possibility of developing it.

Recognizable Symptoms

CD elicits many opportunities for misdiagnosis. Be careful not to mistake it for more common lookalike conditions that are far less serious. Although the following symptoms don't necessarily equate to CD, they are sometimes present:

- lack of standard social skills, such as greeting, maintaining a conversation, listening, behaving in a socially acceptable manner, and taking into account the needs of others; at the more extreme levels, sufferers may be unable to form or maintain close relationships or resolve interpersonal problems
- mood disorders, such as anxiety or depression
- hyperactivity as defined by excess motor activity, such as squirming, fidgeting, or pacing; manifestations can be age-related (little kids might do a lot of extra running, climbing, jumping, whereas a hyperactive 18-year-old would be more likely to display excess fidgeting)
- impulsivity or the tendency to make snap decisions and act on them without regard for consequences; it becomes a problem when the frequency is high and/or the consequences harmful
- adolescent antisocial behaviors that aren't accounted for by other disorders

If sudden onset occurs, suspect other possibilities. If, however, a student exhibits consistent chronic disruptive behavior patterns that aren't diagnosed as other disorders, suspect CD. One symptom is not enough, but two or more exhibited consistently over a period of months is cause for further investigation. Watch and listen for the following additional symptoms:

- aggressive and disruptive behavior patterns (can start as early as first grade and is considered an antecedent or predictor of teenage delinquency); may willfully bully or hurt others
- shows no guilt, remorse, or regard for others' feelings
- may hurt or kill animals
- lies, steals, then wonders why people won't trust them
- lacks empathy

Students with CD may be physically cruel to people and animals, have little or no regard for others' feelings, and exhibit a high incidence of lying, stealing, and peer aggression. Often they have a misperception that others are threatening them when this is not the case. CD sufferers may be chronic bullies, even fighting with weapons. They fail to link up cause and effect (e.g., lying and then not understanding why people don't trust them). They steal without conscience, blame others for their troubles, and cannot acknowledge other people's perspectives because the only view that exists for them is their own. Since they experience the world as outside of their control, anything bad is someone else's fault.

WHAT YOU CAN DO

Early intervention is critical. CD can be evident as early as three or four years of age and, in some cases, even as early as two. The age to intervene is before kindergarten, not when the child has gone on to become a juvenile offender. When you observe the signs of CD over a period of months, it's time for a strong intervention. Do not lock horns with CD sufferers; you will lose. In their minds, they're always right. They feel little or no guilt and no social conscience. But keep in mind that there are things you can do to accommodate the situation.

It is obvious that these students' social operating system is clearly not up to the task of the school's social environment, so it will have to be strengthened dramatically. (Strategies for doing so are discussed in Chapter 2 and in the next section of this chapter.) Do not get sidetracked in pursuing your plan. Here are the essentials:

1. Believe that it will work; know that the brain can and will change with appropriate interventions.

2. Build a team, and make a plan so that every person is on the same page.

3. Focus on building the operating system. In this case, focus on managing states, theory of mind, affiliation skills, social reasoning and developing the student's ability to evaluate potential rewards (although not physical rewards) by taking action.

4. Always maintain relationships throughout the process.

5. Be positive and patient. This will take time.

This is a serious disorder with significant consequences. Do not attempt to treat children suspected to be suffering from CD alone. A response team approach is essential. Involve parents, school administrators, mental health professionals, and sometimes the students themselves.

Remember that this is a brain disorder. You'll need to be smart. Often individuals with CD play the blame game and convince people around them that another party is causing the problem. They may come across as smart and believable, but they are generally highly manipulative. Their blame game works brilliantly to keep concerned individuals off balance. As various parties begin to suspect each other of mistreating students with CD, progress is stalled. You'll need a united front. As mentioned earlier, it helps to get school administrators, psychiatrists, parole officers, parents, and teachers involved, and follow the process outlined in Table 5.2. Have everyone sit down and talk together so that the student in question cannot play one person or group off another.

Use Behavioral Interventions

Before modifying someone else's behavior, first look at your own. Remember to stay focused and patient. Take care of your own stress levels. Students with CD require you to build a relationship with them in a slow, positive manner. This relationship will help you succeed in your goals for them and allow them to buy into your mission.

Avoid engaging in a power struggle with students with CD. Do not engage in verbal confrontations. Use nonthreatening body language, and avoid constant criticism. Be sure to find and focus on the positive behavior that these students exhibit. Offer them increased control over the environment. Empowered with the perception of choice, they will display better behaviors because it lowers stress. Give the students choices (that you have preapproved), offer jobs (that involve things, not people), and teach anger management (e.g., "Pause and count to 10."). Also, offer avenues for being artistic, like writing or creating artwork, which help reduce stress and increase the perception of control.

Table 5.2	Organize a Response Team

- Set a time to meet regularly with the response team.
- Make it a practice not to rely on information from the sufferer that is unchecked and/or unconfirmed.
- Do not include the student in these discussions.
- Do, however, subsequently share with the student the plan established in the meetings.
- Consider both psychological (behavior modification) and physical (drug therapy) interventions when devising the plan. Seek professional medical advice.
- Always include emotional intelligence skills in your curriculum. Teens who participated in a behavior management intervention in first grade were significantly less likely than nonparticipants to start smoking or to engage in antisocial behavior during middle school.

Develop a Plan

Get help as soon as possible. Create a response team, involving all interested parties, and make a plan that includes agreeable action items for dealing with the learner's disruptive behavior patterns. Deal with one behavior at a time using behavior-modification techniques. With a plan in place, you're less likely to overreact or be sucked into the learner's emotional whirlpool. If you prepare for it in advance, they will be less likely to suck you into their negative energy. Teach students with CD emotional intelligence skills to manage the power of their emotions. You don't want to intensify the situation; rather, your goal ought to be to maintain consistent expectations and to de-escalate problem situations when they occur. The following relevant questions ought to be asked by the team:

- What response is appropriate when the student disrupts class or incessantly annoys others?
- What response is appropriate when the student gets into a fight?
- What if he or she brings a weapon to school?
- What should we do when he or she throws a major temper tantrum?
- What response is called for if the student verbally threatens to commit suicide, hurt others, or run away?

Provide a Positive Environment

Keep the environment positive for students with CD. Surround them with optimistic, affirming peers. Also, increase their physical activity. Movement and exercise can up-regulate serotonin, which can increase cognitive flexibility (Chaouloff, 1989). Remember to frequently monitor their progress and that the journey to success is a long, patient one.

Don't Assume the Sufferer Is Being Truthful

Individuals suffering from CD consistently lie. Do not buy into their stories without substantial corroborated evidence.

Be Specific With Requests

Select only one or two specific inappropriate behaviors that you wish to target. Rather than requesting the learner to "be good," try encouraging him or her to "follow my directions, please."

Be Consistent

It is important that the youngster with CD does not receive mixed messages from school and home or from different caregivers. Make sure that everyone is on board with the plan and using it appropriately. Provide a structured environment with predictable consequences. Consistent reinforcement builds new patterns of behaviors.

Grant Privileges Rather Than Rewards

When using a behavior-modification approach (based on rewards and punishment), use privileges, rather than monetary or physical rewards, to reinforce appropriate behaviors.

Share the Plan With the Student

The plan should be simple and straightforward so that the student can easily understand it. If the student can read, he or she should have a written copy of the plan. If appropriate for the age, have the student sign an agreement or "behavior contract."

Seek Professional Advice

A behavior contract alone is not the treatment answer for this serious disorder. Strong intervention at home is also needed. Family therapy with a psychologist or psychiatrist can be useful in improving parent-child dynamics. Avoid tackling the subject of therapy with your input alone. As suggested earlier, create a response team (consisting of parents, teachers, paraprofessionals, etc.). Therapy is ideal when it is structured and focused on developing the needed skills of listening, empathy, and effective problem solving. A psychiatrist may also prescribe drug therapy if he or she deems it necessary. CD is a serious disorder that cannot be alleviated by a few kind words. If you have just a couple of these kids in your school, the staff can solve this. But if your school has a dozen or more, you'll need to bring in a team trained for this. A company called Therapeutic Options can train school staff to deal effectively with kids who suffer from CD.

Strive for Early Detection

Stay alert to patterns (e.g., chronic fighting) that may indicate a problem. If you ignore the symptoms and signs, a child's silent plea for help goes unheard. So you should document the problems as they arise. Cite the specifics of the event (e.g., date, time, behavior, response, any extenuating circumstances) in a notebook or journal. If the learner's behavior continues to be persistently inappropriate, even after you've set down clear expectations and ground rules, notify parents and the school counselor. Interventions are far more effective when administered in third or fourth grade versus high school.

Provide Nutritional Support

Remind parents that nutrition is an important component in regulating brain chemistry and behavior. Foods affect brain chemistry in many ways. For example, milk, turkey, and avocadoes all contain an essential amino acid called tryptophan, which is a natural calming agent that people get from food but cannot manufacture themselves. Consuming whole grains, oatmeal, granola, pasta, rice, and potatoes balance neural activity.

REVISITING THE STUDENT

"Joshua," one of the learners introduced in the pretest at the front of the book, is the student who fits the profile for CD. Like the others, Joshua is unique—he exhibits a pattern of symptoms that are associated with a specific disorder. However, some of these symptoms can be observed in other conditions as well. This is why you want to look for patterns rather than isolated behaviors. To help you remember what's important in assessing students with CD, take a moment, relax, and focus on the photo, the symptoms, and the key points of this chapter.

Symptoms

- Inappropriate emotional outbursts with random acts of destruction
- Consistently hurtful toward peers—swats, hits, and verbally intimidates
- Refuses to follow directions directly; consistently challenges authority
- Loud and aggressive communication patterns, often taunting the teacher and using vulgar language
- Unwilling to participate with others in normal social activities
- Is prone to lie

SUPPLEMENTAL RESOURCES

Books

The Biology of Violence, by Debra Niehoff

Change Your Brain, Change Your Life, by Daniel G. Amen

Conduct Disorders: The Latest Assessment and Treatment, by Mark Eddy

Disruptive Behavior Disorders in Children, by Elizabeth Conneley

Ghosts From the Nursery, by Robin Karr-Morse and Meredith Wiley

Savage Spawn: Reflections on Violent Children, by Jonathan Kellerman

Web sites

American Academy of Child and Adolescent Psychiatry: www.aacap.org

Internet Mental Health: www.mentalhealth.com

6

The Demotivated Learner

Stress Disorders

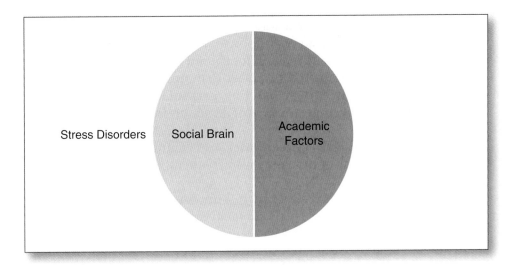

You may have seen kids who are hyporesponsive. In Chapter 4, we noted that these are often the kids with learned helplessness. Students may also be hyperresponsive, suffering from a chronic or traumatic stress disorder. (Chronic stress is also known as distress.) The most common cause of academic demotivation is chronic exposure to distress and/or threat (whether at home, in the community, or at school) without sufficient coping skills to handle it. Distress can be physical or emotional, and it affects attention, focus, and concentration (Erickson, Drevets, & Schulkin, 2003).

Stress is a physiological response to a perception of a lack of control over an aversive situation or person. The brain responds to distress (e.g., elevated stress levels over time) by hypersecretion of cortisol, which can have devastating effects on the brain. Prevalence of children in America with chronic or acute stress disorders is 18 to 20 percent (Perry & Pollard, 1997). In fact, the largest group of stress disorder victims is school-age children.

Stress disorders, which affect test scores, behaviors, and social decisions, encompass a large class of conditions, including general anxiety disorder, bipolar disorder, major depression, attachment disorder, posttraumatic stress disorder (PTSD), learned helplessness, and seasonal affective disorder.

Stress can be a result of something mundane like long-term irrelevant curriculum, sedentary instruction, or teaching/learning style mismatches. Or it can be the result of something more intense like abuse, hunger, and peer violence. For many students, school is a dangerous place. And when perceived as such, a learner's instinct to survive overrides the motivation for academic success. When this evolutionary response to threat or distress occurs time after time, the learner's brain ultimately suffers. Eventually, a maladaptive response to even everyday stressors may result.

While moderate short-term stress, in most cases, is conducive to learning and a healthy immune response, chronic distress is debilitating. And unfortunately, children are not spared from this rule. Stress has a cumulative effect—more stress equates to more impulsivity. The body undergoes allostasis, in which baseline cortisol levels are increased. High cortisol levels become toxic over time, and prolonged allostatic load suppresses one's overall health, mental endurance, and quickness of memory retrieval (Lupien, McEwan, Gunnar, & Heim, 2009). Stress over long periods of time may also create lifelong health problems (McEwen, 2008).

Unfortunately, the brain cannot successfully sustain such high levels of stress. Chronic or acute stress levels cut the brain's new neuron production by up to 50 percent. It is true that we have a fault-tolerant brain, and most of the time we adapt well to daily stress; however, when stress related hormones (known as glucocorticoids) are chronically elevated, learners can become distracted, hurried, sloppy, apathetic, and uninterested in learning. Recent neuroscientific research confirms that, when these excess glucocorticoids are present over an extended period of time, brain cells ultimately die and aging is dramatically accelerated.

UNDERSTANDING THREAT

A threat is an action or event that you perceive will compromise your goals. Threat may come in the form of the playground bully, an abusive parent, or even a teacher who embarrasses students in front of their peers. Threat is an acute state of alarm characterized by some risk and urgency. Threatening occurrences can be divided into two categories: primary activation (a real or immediate threat) and reactivation (a remembered or potential threat).

Primary activation in the classroom setting can occur when a teacher calls on an unprepared student or when a student has to present in front of his or her peers with insufficient preparation. It can also occur in an abusive household, on the way to school, on the playground, or anywhere danger is present. While some neuroscientists, such as Joseph LeDoux, believe that the brain's threat system is activated like an on/off switch, others, such as Paul Whalen, have demonstrated that it works more like a rheostat. Everyone, however, agrees that when threat is perceived, the body prepares itself with a bath of glucocorticoids, among them adrenaline (the fight-or-flight hormone), in an effort to protect itself.

Reactivation occurs when a prior activation of threat or distress is triggered. This can happen in any environment, including a truly safe one. The sound of something slamming down on a desk or the disapproving sight of a hostile classmate or teacher can reactivate a prior intense negative association, triggering the stress response. When this occurs, the amygdala, a midbrain area highly involved in memory and emotion, recreates the past in the mind. We all have triggers that can set us off.

Understanding Distress

Distress is a chronic condition characterized by the release of excess glucocorticoids, including cortisol, the hormone of negative expectations. While in the short run cortisol can be beneficial, over the long haul elevated levels wreak havoc on the body. Distress (chronically high stress levels) narrows perceptual focus, weakens social skills, hampers memory, reduces creativity, weakens the immune system, lessens attentional skills, diminishes enjoyment of learning, and can impair the processing of learning.

As stated previously, stress is the body's response to a perception of loss of control over a situation, person, or event that we believe to be aversive. Keep in mind that it is not the event or experience that causes distress in our lives. It's always about the interaction between the event and our coping skills. That's why there are no stressful schools or stressful jobs, only our experiences of stress that we generate at a school or job. It just feels like an event or person is stressing us out. In reality, our coping skills often are simply insufficient. This situational definition leaves us with a wide variety of potential stressors. Distress has been categorized and explained in the following ways:

Short-term trauma. A single discrete traumatic event, such as the violent death of a school acquaintance, can result in short-term dysfunction in individuals who are otherwise healthy. Common effects include intense bad memories or dreams, emotional numbing, feelings of detachment or unreality, and bodily tension. The victims of short-term trauma usually experience a complete recovery within weeks or months of the occurrence with sufficient counseling and support from friends and family.

Acute stress disorder. This short-term condition (lasting less than a month) is generated by an unusually traumatic event that provokes fear, horror, or helplessness and causes emotional numbing, hyperarousal, severe anxiety, and distressing dreams or recollections of the experience. Like the more chronic condition, posttraumatic stress disorder (or syndrome), acute stress disorder is often seen in soldiers returning from combat, but it is also prevalent in civilians, including children. It can be caused, for example, by a catastrophic natural disaster such as a fire, earthquake, or tornado or by physical violence such as a rape, robbery, kidnapping, shooting, bombing, or gang activity. The condition is characterized by panic reactions, mental confusion, dissociation, severe insomnia, suspiciousness, and an inability to manage even basic self-care, work, and social activities. If the symptoms last longer than one month, a diagnosis of PTSD might be indicated.

Posttraumatic stress disorder. This is the chronic version of acute stress disorder. The two conditions share the same criteria for diagnosis, except that PTSD symptoms extend beyond a month. PTSD is also caused by severe trauma from, for example, a natural or man-made disaster and is characterized by persistent reexperiencing of the traumatic event, avoidance of stimuli associated with the trauma, emotional numbing, and hyperarousal or severe anxiety. The condition may overlap with one or more other psychiatric disorders such as depression, alcohol/drug abuse, and panic disorder.

The most extreme cases are referred to as complex PTSD or disorder of extreme stress. Complex PTSD is generally seen in individuals who have been exposed to prolonged trauma, especially during childhood, such as repeated childhood sexual abuse. These individuals are often also diagnosed with other serious psychiatric conditions such as a dissociative disorder, borderline personality disorder, or antisocial personality disorder. The behavioral difficulties they may experience include impulsivity, aggression, sexual acting out, eating or sleeping dysfunction, alcohol/drug abuse, and/or other self-destructive actions. Extreme emotional difficulties (e.g., intense rage, depression, panic) and mental difficulties (e.g., fragmented thoughts, dissociation, amnesia) are also prevalent.

IMPACT

The National Center for Posttraumatic Stress Disorder estimates that 3 to 15 percent of girls and 1 to 6 percent of boys meet the full criteria for PTSD (Schnurr et al., 2003). The single hardest-hit group of trauma victims is children. They have far greater vulnerability to trauma and less resiliency than adults. Children who witness domestic abuse, are rape victims, or experience sexual and/or verbal abuse are categorized as part of a high-risk group likely to have PTSD (Ackerman, Newton, McPherson, Jones, & Dykman, 1998). As these children enter adolescence and adulthood, the symptoms resulting from the trauma are often amplified by additional trauma. Potential threats are many and varied. They may stem from abusive parents, violent neighborhoods, inadequate childcare, chronic incidents of bullying in transit to school or at school, unsafe school environments, or even a single abusive classmate.

PTSD was originally diagnosed in combat veterans, but it has also been seen in a disproportionate number of rape and incest victims, survivors of natural or man-made disasters (e.g., hurricanes, tornadoes, flooding), and witnesses of extreme violence. People with PTSD often exhibit other psychological difficulties as well—particularly depression, substance abuse, or an anxiety disorder. Treatment success increases when comorbid conditions are appropriately diagnosed and treated first or in conjunction with PTSD.

Demographics

Of course, not every traumatized person experiences PTSD; however, we do know that in noncombat situations, PTSD affects both genders, with a higher incidence reported in females. In animal models, interestingly, the more outgoing and aggressive the rats, the more likely they were to experience threat and distress.

Commentary

An important myth to dispel is that PTSD and acute stress disorder only occur in war veterans. In fact, children are the largest group impacted. Children simply don't have the coping skills needed to deal with extreme conditions. Symptoms are usually evident within three months of the trauma, but onset sometimes doesn't occur until years later. The course of the illness varies. Some people recover within six months; others have a longer battle. In some cases, the condition may be chronic.

Likely Causes

Traumatic Environmental Conditions

Traumatic conditions, especially early in a child's life, can profoundly impact personality. When internalized and reinforced, these events remain forever painful and present. Early parental loss, for example, accompanied by the lack of a supportive relationship subsequent to the loss (an external stress-reducing factor) could easily set off a series of circumstances that ultimately result in acute stress disorder or PTSD. Other traumatic environmental conditions include a poverty cycle; abandonment; abduction; emotional, sexual, and/or physical abuse; parental fighting; feeling trapped in an unhappy marriage or in a despised job or career; political violence; and ethnic rivalries. With no hope, the individual eventually gives up searching for solutions.

Prenatal Distress

Some nonhuman research indicates that prenatal stress may predispose infants to having a more difficult temperament pattern. Attentional disorders, neuromotor deficits, diminished cognition, and fewer play behaviors may be evidenced.

Unsafe Schools

Many schools are simply not safe for children. Surprisingly, metal detectors and on-site security officers do not create the feeling of safety. Rather, they can trigger the threat response. A sense of safety is better generated by a schoolwide commitment to the caring, nurturing, and acceptance of children. Fostering a threat-free school environment should be a top priority.

High Resting Heart Rate

Significant cardiovascular liability is a prominent feature in children with PTSD. In one sample of children with PTSD, about 85 percent had a high resting heart rate (greater than 94 beats per minute) and about 40 percent had resting rates of greater than 100 beats per minute. An age-comparable group of normal children exhibits an average resting heart rate of 84 beats per minute.

Frontal-Lobe Dysfunction

It is common for people experiencing acute stress to be overly aroused, short-tempered, irritable, anxious, and tense. They cannot prioritize their schedule; they cannot tell the difference between important and unimportant objectives or urgent and nonurgent situations. Without a way to prioritize, they become victims. They take on too much, have too many irons in the fire, and can't organize the slew of self-inflicted demands and pressures clamoring for their attention. These choices are all functions of the executive decision-making area of the frontal lobe.

Distortion

A distorted belief system or view of the world can cause unending stress for an individual (e.g., "The world is a threatening place," "People will find out I'm a pretender," "We have to be perfect at all times.").

Family Life

Children in low-income families have many disadvantages. They often are subjected to moving and getting evicted (Federman et al., 1996). Such mobility issues cause them to have fewer social ties. The chaos and disruption, along with worries about money, create a stressful environment for the entire family. In addition, household income is inversely related to exposure to familial violence, which can significantly impact chronic and acute stress levels (Emery & Laumann-Billings, 1998). Being exposed to more stressors, and that last for long periods of time, results in children from low-income backgrounds having fewer coping skills than children from higher socioeconomic backgrounds.

Brain Areas Involved

The brain adapts to chronic stressors with either of two extremes. There is habituation and eventual desensitization to stress (numbness). These students are often listless, apathetic, and unresponsive. Alternatively, there is hypervigilance, which is characterized by edgy, suspicious, and overreactive behavior.

Autonomic Nervous System

The brain directs both the sympathetic system (in emergency conditions) and the parasympathetic system (in normal conditions). Both of these implicit systems activate and suppress bodily functions that help us respond appropriately to life. Chronic threat and distress, however, can ultimately alter the healthy functioning of these systems. The source of the problem is not a busy, stressful life, but our capacity to remember and create. The overstimulation that occurs in response to dozens of feared or imagined future events further complicates the ability to separate genuine from illusory threats.

One study recently found how distress affects neurons in rats (Brown, Henning, & Wellman, 2005). The group exposed to distress significantly changed the growth and shape of their neurons. The withered neurons were taken from a rat's prefrontal cortex after being exposed to just one week of 10 minutes a day of stress. Stressors force the brain to withdraw its growth resources, and that hurts learning.

Hypothalamus

The response to distress starts here as a four-part process: (1) stress activates the hypothalamus, which then releases corticotropin-releasing factor (CRF); (2) when CRF reaches the pituitary gland, it triggers the release of the adrenocorticotropin hormones (ACTH); (3) the ACTH, in turn, reach the adrenals and stimulate the production of the stress hormones, known as glucocorticoids (such as cortisol), into the blood-stream; and (4) these hormones control the body's use of sugar, raise blood pressure, boost energy, and temporarily strengthen immune responses. We might say that the adrenals are "ground zero" for the stress response.

In response to distress, the adrenal glands secrete two primary chemicals. Epinephrine (adrenaline) acts within seconds but cannot be sustained, while glucocorticoids (steroid hormones) last for minutes, hours, or days but aren't activated as quickly. These biochemical responses to threat also stimulate the pancreas to release its own hormone, glucagon, which provides the sustained energy necessary to deal with stress.

Reticular Activating System

This area of the brain acts as an orienting mechanism that helps us identify a particular direction for a response. When threatened, it initiates the cascade of chemical reactions that mobilize the mind and body for preservation.

Hippocampus

This crescent-shaped structure, located within the temporal lobes in the lower middle part of the brain, may be the most susceptible to acute or chronic distress. For example, some loss in size of the hippocampus has been noted in PTSD cases. Clearly, a typical stressor experienced in a normal day does not constitute acute distress. Rather, it is four to eight weeks or more of acute exposure that has been shown to ultimately suppress dendritic growth and neuron maintenance in the hippocampus region— specific to episodic and semantic memory. Adrenal steroids—released in response to stress—inhibit cell proliferation in the dentate gyrus during the early postnatal period and in adulthood. It is not clear whether the cell loss is permanent or is a reversible atrophy. Today scientists are convinced, however, that our brain can grow new cells, and enrichment seems to accelerate the process.

Caudate Nucleus and Putamen

Chronic psychosocial conflict decreases dopamine transporter binding sites in motor-related brain areas, resulting in a reduction in locomotor activity.

Genes

Mice lacking CRF receptors have been shown to exhibit more distress and anxious behaviors than do normal mice.

Cerebral Blood Flow

Adults with PTSD exhibit increased cerebral blood flow in anterior paralimbic regions and orbitofrontal and anterior temporal regions.

Frontal Lobes

Studies implicate dysfunction of the medial prefrontal cortex (subcallosal gyrus and anterior cingulate). Activation in these brain areas may be a result of a reactivation occurrence in PTSD sufferers. Under threat, there is a decrease in blood flow to the anterior dorsal area of the frontal lobes (higher, up front), which manages executive function, short-term memory, planning, thinking, and creativity. There is also an increase in blood flow to the anterior ventral frontal lobes (lower, up front), which are used for emotional processing. In short, the greater the exposure to threat, the less blood flows to the areas of the brain needed for thinking and learning. These changes increase the likelihood that the distressed student will be flooded with emotions, making him or her less able to resolve the problem at hand.

Recognizable Symptoms

A highly distressed or somewhat traumatized student will generally react in one of two ways. The brain responds to distress by hypersecretion of glucocorticoids. The net effect is a habituation and eventual desensitization to stress (numbness). The opposite reaction is hypervigilance. Hypervigilant students are always on red alert for danger, scanning the environment for verbal or nonverbal cues of impending threat. A student who is severely distressed does not snap out of it quickly. Count on it to take some time.

The following symptom clusters are associated with acute stress disorder and PTSD:

- recurring intrusive recollections of the traumatic event, such as dreams and flashbacks
- persistent avoidance of stimuli associated with the trauma or numbing of general responsiveness
- persistent increased arousal characterized by hypervigilance, increased startle response, sleep difficulties, irritability, anxiety, and physiological hyperactivity; students may lose interest in things they used to enjoy, have trouble feeling affectionate, feel irritable and more aggressive than before, or even violent—all conditions that severely inhibit learning

The symptoms of acute distress disorder and PTSD can range from mild to severe. Sufferers may become easily irritated or have violent outbursts. In severe cases they may have trouble working or socializing. In general, the symptoms seem to be worse if the event that triggered them was initiated by a person (e.g., rape) as opposed to a disaster (e.g., flood).

Unfortunately, ordinary classroom events can serve as reminders of the trauma and trigger flashbacks or intrusive images. Flashbacks can cause a temporary distortion of reality in sufferers that may last for a period of seconds, hours, or occasionally days. A flashback, which consists of images, sounds, smells, and/or feelings, can be so real in the sufferer's mind that he or she actually relives the trauma each time the flashback occurs.

Abuse

Typical symptoms and behaviors in the abused child include acting out, shy and anxious behavior patterns, and learning problems. Abuse victims regularly exhibit low frustration tolerance, weak social skills, and low task orientation.

Look for physical signs of abuse, such as unlikely or suspicious bandages, sunglasses worn to hide swelling, or long-sleeved shirts on warm days. Listen for signals of stress in the voice. Abused girls may exhibit abnormally high motor activity or bursts of physical energy. They also may be more resistant to cooperation, more impulsive, and more anxious. Traumatized children are usually less descriptive and verbal in conversations; they also talk less about themselves and about feelings. They are usually hypervigilant—ever on the lookout for potential danger and sensitive to nonverbal cues. Boys generally externalize their exposure to trauma and become more aggressive or isolated. Girls typically internalize the effects by dissociation or simply freezing.

Attachment Disorder

All or most of the following symptoms/behaviors are present in the child suffering from attachment disorder:

- *manipulation:* superficially engaging or charming (a control tactic)
- *eye contact avoidance:* especially when on parents' terms
- *inappropriate affection:* indiscriminately affectionate with strangers or, conversely, not inclined to give and receive affection (not cuddly)
- *need for tight control:* extreme control battles often manifested in covert or sneaky ways
- *self-destructive:* also of others, animals, and objects; accident prone; may steal
- *hoarding behavior:* gorging on food and abnormal eating patterns
- *preoccupation with danger:* attracted to fire, blood, and gore

- *impulse control problems:* cannot internalize cause-and-effect logic; frequently hyperactive; lacking conscience
- *developmental delays:* learning lags and speech disorders common; abnormal speech patterns
- *compulsive lying:* chronically lies even about obvious or crazy things
- *weak social skills:* poor peer relationships or isolation
- *inappropriate verbal communication:* persistent nonsense questions and incessant chatter
- *demanding:* inappropriately demanding, impatient, and clingy
- *parental hostility:* caretakers likely to appear hostile and angry

WHAT YOU CAN DO

Chances are pretty good that students dealing with threat or chronic distress will seem out of sorts. They will be coping, not thriving. You can make a difference by providing a positive learning environment with consistent daily routines and expectations. Model good stress management skills and, when appropriate, incorporate into lesson plans such activities as deep breathing, stretching, visualization, goal setting, good eating habits, problem solving, and exercise. Distressed learners will likely need more of a boost to get them into the learning groove and keep them engaged. Here are some ways you can help reduce their stress:

- Provide opportunities for personal control and decision making.
- Offer predictability through overviews, routines, rituals, and reviews.
- Help students find positive outlets for their frustration.
- Reinforce the belief that conditions can and will improve despite temporary setbacks.
- Model good stress management and problem-solving skills.

These kids demonstrate clearly that their social operating system is not up to the task of the school's social environment. It will have to be strengthened. (Strategies for doing so are discussed in Chapter 2 and in the next section of this chapter.) Do not get sidetracked in pursuing your plan. Here are the essentials:

1. Believe that it will work; know that the brain can and will change with appropriate interventions.

2. Build a team, and make a plan so that every person is on the same page.

3. Focus on building the operating system. As you might guess, these students need support in coping skills, or managing their emotional

states. This is one of the core components of a social operating system. Affiliation also may need to be strengthened.

4. Always maintain relationships throughout the process.

5. Be positive and patient. This will take time.

The strategies presented in this section can help turn what might at first feel like a hopeless situation into a constructive one. They represent generally sound teaching practices, so they'll benefit all of your students. However, when incorporated into a consistent classroom routine, they can have an especially powerful effect on distressed learners. Merely discovering that success at school is a realistic possibility can be a life-changing experience for these kids. Many successful adults raised in troubled homes or faced with early life trauma attribute their achievements later in life to the support of a caring teacher who helped them cope with their stress and channel their energy productively. The top two strategies are to build relationships and to build hope. Without those two, students have little chance to succeed.

Of course, these strategies don't need to be implemented all at once. Initiate one at a time if you wish. Soon they'll become a natural part of your daily classroom routine. It is important to make it reasonably easy for learners to experience success in your classroom. Be sure that your expectations are realistic, clearly communicated, and consistently reinforced. When students achieve a goal, validate their success. Once the powerful cycle of empowerment/motivation/achievement is set in motion, students learn that they can channel their energy into either positive or negative directions. They come to understand that it is their own daily decisions that ultimately determine the course of their life.

Personalize Your Attention

When interacting with students, use their first names. Make sure that your first and last interactions of the day are positive. Students tend to recall the first and last things you say. If they are greeted with a frown or complaint day after day, soon they'll associate school with drudgery and negativity.

Incorporate More Physical Activity

Start the day with a movement activity to get the blood flowing, and regularly break up seatwork with physical activity throughout the day. Facilitate a stretching or deep breathing session, a group assignment, or some walk-and-talk time. Games, relays, experiments, or moving to music are other ways to get physical. Teach students the stress management value of slow, deep breathing and stretching, which increase oxygen to the brain and body. Also encourage emotional release and stress reduction through art, creative writing, drama, and music.

Get Connected

Give students ample opportunities to interact with each other. Take a few moments yourself to check in with students in a brief, personal way. Share something you enjoyed over the weekend—a new discovery, a funny story, or a personal learning experience. The relationship that a teacher establishes with his or her students is an important factor in teaching and learning success. Journaling and peer discussions are also effective strategies for helping distressed learners identify and cope with their trauma/stress.

Establish Routines

A ritual is a dependable event (e.g., reciting the Pledge of Allegiance each morning). A routine is a string of rituals. All of us follow rituals and routines every day, either consciously or unconsciously (e.g., when getting ready for work). Classroom rituals and routines help anchor students—a practice that is especially important for distressed learners. Provide regular overviews so students can anticipate the learning objectives for the day, week, month, and year. Make the rituals fun and meaningful. For example, you might incorporate a daily three-minute drawing and sharing session.

Incorporate Stress–Reduction Strategies

Teach students ways to regulate their own stress levels, such as relaxation techniques, yoga, singing, artwork, taking a breather, conflict resolution, managing self-talk, visualization, and physical exercise or movement.

Restore Motivation

Distressed students often suffer from lack of motivation as a result of feeling underempowered or overpowered by others. Offset this problem with the following five brain-compatible teaching principles:

Eliminate the threat. Avoid placing unrealistic demands on students, such as giving assignments without the necessary resources and support to accomplish them. Do not make statements in a threatening tone. Avoid embarrassing students in front of their peers, punishing them, putting them on the spot, or calling on them when they didn't volunteer. Honor students' answers whether they're correct or not. Be sensitive to students' feelings.

Encourage goal setting. Encourage students to set daily, weekly, and long-term goals. Check in with them on a regular basis, provide feedback, and validate their progress. For example, ask students to share their goals with classmates by posting them as timelines or charts. Public recognition is a great motivator and strategy for reinforcing progress. Once distressed learners set a goal, do everything in your power to help them succeed.

Activate emotions. Engage learners in creative projects that incorporate drawing, painting, music making, building, dancing, and performing. Engage learners with movement activities such as relays, games, stretching, Simon Says, walks, and energizers. Encourage a feeling of purpose through meaningful projects such as service work, yearbooks, community competitions, journal keeping, directories, and political activism.

Increase feedback. Students are typically starved for feedback. The traditional primary mechanisms for feedback—test results and semester grades—are not sufficient in themselves to assist students in reaching coursework objectives. Increasing the means for providing it can increase feedback. It does not have to be given by the teacher every time. Peer collaboration and teamwork can play an important role in the feedback process. A basic guideline is to make sure students receive some form of feedback every half hour. You can help achieve this by incorporating peer editing, self-recorded audiotapes, wall progress charts, checklists, student check-ins and reviews, friendly competitions, group process and observation, cross-age tutoring, computer-assisted instruction, and peer and self-reflection opportunities. Tie your feedback to students' personal goals, being sure to offset constructive criticism with positive reinforcement of progress.

Create a positive learning climate. Provide ample acknowledgment of individual and group accomplishments and efforts. Increase the number and types of classroom celebrations and team activities. Keep up with current events, and encourage learners to do the same. Incorporate real-life experiences into the curriculum as frequently as you can. Little rituals, such as celebrating the completion of a new unit with a group success chant, can go a long way toward warming the classroom climate and reinforcing positive accomplishments.

REVISITING THE STUDENT

"Mary," one of the learners introduced in the pretest at the front of the book, is the student who fits the profile for chronic threat and distress. Like the others, Mary is unique—she exhibits a pattern of symptoms that are associated with a specific disorder. However, some of these symptoms can be observed in other conditions as well. This is why you want to look for patterns rather than isolated behaviors. To help you remember what's important in assessing students with a stress disorder, take a moment, relax, and focus on the photo, the symptoms, and the key points of this chapter.

Symptoms

- Seems to be edgy and on alert
- Trance-like state is common; doesn't snap out of it quickly
- Appears bored and disconnected
- Short-term memory loss and inability to prioritize
- Makes careless errors in schoolwork
- Decreased social contact
- Doesn't remember "where" questions
- Loss of creativity and poor concentration
- Seems to be sick more often than peers

SUPPLEMENTAL RESOURCES

Books

Active Learning: 101 Strategies, by Mel Silberman

EMDR: The Breakthrough Therapy, by Francine Shapiro

Motivation and Learning, by Spence Rogers, Jim Ludington, and Shari Graham

Why Zebras Don't Get Ulcers, by Robert Sapolsk

Web sites

Anxiety Disorders Association of America: www.adaa.org

American Psychiatric Association: www.psych.org

CyberPsych: www.cyberpsych.org

International Society for Traumatic Stress Studies: www.istss.org

National Center for Posttraumatic Stress Disorder: www.ncptsd.va.gov

National Institute of Mental Health: www.nimh.nih.gov

7

The Troubled Learner

Depression

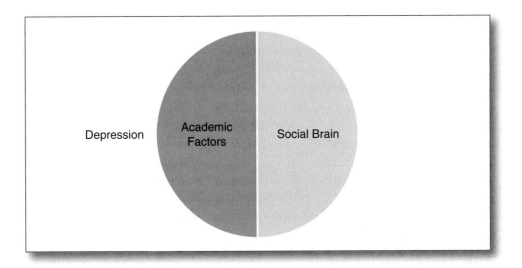

The classic notion of depression is that the person who suffers from it is sad and usually an adult. Get ready for what the research now tells us: teens experience depression a great deal more than we ever thought, and they don't always show symptoms of sadness. Depression is a chronic and serious mood disorder that is pervasive and intense, and attacks both the mind and body. The person feels helpless and hopeless and may express these feelings with anger, irritability, and frustration. The most common type of depression presents itself with the loss of enjoyment, anger, and sleep and weight abnormalities. The most effective therapy is behavioral (e.g., exercise, socialization), cognitive, and pharmaceutical.

This highly disruptive condition typically impairs academic performance, job performance, and family life, and it can sometimes lead to suicide. The following five categories of depression are commonly used to diagnose the severity of the condition:

- *Major depressive disorder:* This most common form of depression is characterized by at least five major symptoms, including melancholy, loss of energy, impaired concentration, insomnia, hypersomnia, anxiety, and diminished libido. Either through single or recurrent episodes, this form of depression can reach mild, moderate, or severe levels and can hinder occupational, social, and interpersonal relationships. Sufferers who experience recurrent episodes are more likely to have suicidal thoughts than those who experience a single episode. Recent official estimates in the United States indicate that by age 19, approximately 28 percent of youth will have experienced a major depressive episode (Lewinsohn, Rohde, & Seeley, 1998).

- *Dysthymic disorder:* This milder form of depression lasts a minimum of two years. It is the second most common type of depression, but because sufferers tend to accept its relatively mild symptoms as "normal," it often goes overlooked, undiagnosed, and untreated. Typically, dysthymia begins at age seven or eight and can last a lifetime. Severity increases with recurrent episodes. Findings indicate that youngsters with this disorder have significant impairment and use more mental health services than those with major depression (González-Tejera et al., 2005).

- *Bipolar disorder:* Formerly known as manic-depressive disorder, this severe and chronic "roller coaster" illness has a strong genetic link and is characterized by extreme highs and lows. The symptoms are similar to those of major depression, with certain variations such as mania and intense mood swings. Bipolar disorder is just as crippling as major depression, even during euphoric phases. Some believe that the longer bipolar disorder goes untreated, the more damage is done to the brain.

- *Seasonal affective disorder:* This form of depression follows seasonal rhythms, with symptoms occurring in the winter months and diminishing in spring and summer. Individuals most depressed in the winter are among the most elated in the summer. Those with this type of depression are often treated with increasing exposure to artificial light boxes in the winter, improved social contact, and exercise. Some researchers believe that this may be a mild version of bipolar disorder.

- *Posttraumatic stress disorder* (*PTSD*): This is the chronic version of acute stress disorder (see Chapter 6). Common environmental triggers for PTSD include natural disasters, vehicle accidents, life-threatening illnesses or medical procedures, physical abuse, or sudden death of a loved one. Typically, children with PTSD show a combination of problems, including impulsivity, distractibility and attention problems (due to hypervigilance), dysphoria, emotional numbing, social avoidance, dissociation, sleep problems, aggressive behavior (often reenactment play), school failure, and regressed or delayed development. Students with bona fide PTSD symptoms are often labeled as having attention deficit hyperactivity disorder, depression, oppositional defiant disorder, conduct disorder, separation anxiety, or a specific phobia because it shares many symptoms with these conditions.

IMPACT

Only a licensed professional (e.g., pediatrician, psychologist, neurologist, psychiatrist, clinical social worker), in consultation with the *Diagnostic and Statistical Manual of Mental Disorders* (American Psychiatric Association, 2000), can make the diagnosis that a child, teen, or adult has depression. In some cases, a clinical diagnosis of depression is possible in children by age five or six, although people who live in poverty are especially difficult to diagnose because of other contributing factors. Diagnosis is often delayed until unusual problems (e.g., relocation, exposure to trauma, parental separation) in school are sorted out. Diagnosis requires observation of indices in two of three settings: home, school, and office.

Typically, major depressive episodes last 9 to 12 months. More than 80 percent of people with depression improve with treatment by the end of the first year. Even if untreated, the symptoms may disappear temporarily, but the risk remains substantial that other adverse behaviors (e.g., drug abuse, suicide attempts, excessive consumption of caffeine, sleep disorders) will occur. Not all kids who are depressed have clinical major depression, but all episodes of depression should be taken seriously. About one in ten kids who develop major depression will commit suicide (Dervic et al., 2006).

Anxiety is a common symptom of depression, often becoming so severe that sufferers stay in bed to cope with it. This severe level of anxiety is also observed in individuals suffering from an actual anxiety disorder. Anxiety, as well as many other overlapping conditions, often occurs in conjunction with depression.

Demographics

Prevalence of depression varies depending on the type of study, demographics, and adherence to strict definitions. Some interpret the symptoms and contexts differently than others, and symptoms may be masked by other more acute disorders. Temperament, genetics, and environmental causes also play into mental health. Prior to puberty, depression rates are equal among girls and boys; however, the number increases dispropor-tionately for women later. According to the U.S. Surgeon General's mental health report (U.S. Department of Health and Human Services, 1999), one in five children has a mental health disorder. Kids get most distressed from school work (e.g., grades, homework, activities), family issues, and social issues (e.g., gossip, teasing).

Women are more prone to both depression and panic attacks; in fact, twice as many women than men experience depression. However, more men than women suffer from drug and alcohol abuse. And while every-body, including children, can develop the illness, individuals with less education and lower income levels are more vulnerable to it.

Commentary

Depression is serious and should be treated immediately, but identifi-cation and treatment can be difficult since this complex disorder is so often accompanied by overlapping conditions. Some commonly observed comorbid conditions are alcohol/drug abuse, anxiety disorders, social pho-bias, and obsessive-compulsive disorder.

Depression constitutes a high level of challenge to the classroom teacher. You can contribute to the success of learners with depression, but you will need support from others—notably parents and mental health professionals.

Likely Causes

It is important to understand that the etiology of depression is varied. Mixed factors, genetic as well as nongenetic, all come into play. While anti-depressant drugs may alleviate some symptoms, they don't treat the cause. The following are some of the more common explanations for depression.

Chemical Dysregulation

Neuroscientists are unsure whether imbalances in neurotransmitter levels in the brain cause depression or are a result of the depression. You may have heard that serotonin levels are low in people with depression. This is commonly true. However, their brains also have suboptimal levels of norepinephrine and dopamine. The medications prescribed for depres-sion, such as serotonin selective reuptake inhibitors (SSRIs), increase levels of serotonin, often (but not always) resulting in effective treatment of depression for the majority of patients who take them. Unfortunately, there are risks with any medications and the effectiveness wanes over time as the brain adapts to a given drug.

Cytokines

Major depression is associated with the dysfunction of inflammatory mediators called cytokines. Several lines of evidence indicate that brain cytokines, principally interleukin-1beta (IL-1beta) and IL-1 receptor antagonist, may play a role in the biology of major depression, and they might also affect the pathophysiology, somatic consequences, and treatment effectiveness.

Distress

Whether chronic or acute, distress increases the likelihood of depression. Extreme stress may impair the brain's ability to deal with change, further increasing the risk of depression. Ironically, children who are sheltered from life's stressful challenges are also at higher risk for depression. Children need moderately stressful experiences to develop their resiliency—a personal strength that will help them avert depression later in life.

Seasonal Darkness

Current research indicates that seasonal reduction of sunlight can trigger a biochemical reaction in some individuals that may cause loss of energy, decreased activity, increased sadness, and excessive eating and sleeping. This condition is called seasonal affect disorder.

Smoking

Sufferers of major depression are more likely to smoke and to experience difficulty trying to quit. When such individuals do manage to quit, they are at increased risk of experiencing mild to severe states of depression, including full-blown major depression.

Brain Mass Differences

Recent studies on depression have implicated several areas of the brain as having less mass than in healthy subjects. For example, the hippocampus is typically 5 to 12 percent smaller. This is a structure in the temporal lobes that is highly involved with learning and memory. Another structure that is affected is the subgenual prefrontal cortex, a small area located behind the bridge of the nose. In patients with depression, this area has been found to contain an average of 39 to 48 percent less brain tissue. In addition, it was found to be 8 percent less active in individuals with depression compared to unaffected individuals. It also was found to contain 41 percent fewer glial cells.

Malnutrition

Psychological symptoms are often associated with a deficiency in several vitamins and minerals. For example, a balance in thiamin has been shown in several double-blind studies to improve mood (Benton & Donohoe, 1999), and iron deficiency, a particularly common condition in women, is associated with apathy, depression, and rapid fatigue during exercise.

Heredity

Depression and bipolar disorder frequently run in families. Close blood relatives of people with depression are more likely to suffer from the condition than are individuals without such a family member.

Parenting Style

Children's resiliency is influenced by their parent's income levels, parenting style, and other life experiences. Those brought up in a privileged family may have less resiliency in the face of stressful life events. Their pampered lifestyle may leave them with less exposure to stressors and can harbor learned helplessness tendencies. Children who are reared with healthy attachments and exposed to stressors are more likely to be emotionally independent and resilient against life's stressors. They figure out how to cope. In a survey of nearly 1,400 people, the researchers found strong association between emotional reliance and depression (Turner & Avison, 2003).

From the time they are 15 to 54 months old, almost 80 percent of children today spend nearly 20 to 25 hours a week in daycare (Campbell, Spieker, Burchinal, Poe, & The NICHD Early Child Care Research Network, 2006). The lack of appropriate individual attention and excessive random environmental stimulation may cause emotional issues in the future. Times have changed significantly. These numbers are more than double that of two generations ago. Today, it is more common for both parents to work outside the home and send their kids to daycare, whereas in years past one parent tended to stay home full time. Emotional stability begins with the quantity of quality time children receive.

Brain Areas Involved

Figure 7.1 illustrates how a person suffering from depression shows significant underactivity in the prefrontal lobe and temporal lobe in comparison to a healthy, activated brain.

Basal Ganglia

Severe depression occurs more often among individuals with lesions in the basal ganglia—an area containing an abundance of neurotransmitters and receptors.

Cingulate Gyrus

This brain area, located behind the frontal lobes, is often implicated in depression. It is one of the areas removed in a frontal lobotomy—the

Figure 7.1 Comparisons of Activation Patterns: Healthy Brain Versus Depressed Brain

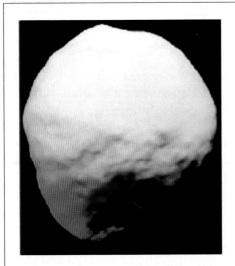 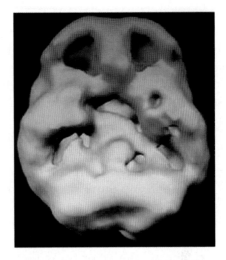

Healthy brain: note the smooth, even activation.

Depressed brain: note the "holes" of inactivity in the frontal and limbic areas.

Source: Images courtesy of Daniel Amen, MD.

controversial surgery that used to be commonly performed in severe cases of depression.

Limbic Area

This deep frontal midbrain area is typically overactive in people with depression. It includes the hypothalamus, thalamus, and olfactory areas, which are involved in bonding, smell, and sexuality. It also includes the amygdala and hippocampus, two structures responsible for memory, emotion, and perception.

Frontal Lobes

The subgenual prefrontal cortex has been shown to be less active and to contain less brain tissue in individuals suffering from depression.

Recognizable Symptoms

One challenge in recognizing depression is that human beings, by nature, have variable moods. We're happy; we're sad; we're anxious; we're calm. Considering the number of daily factors capable of influencing mood, such as hunger, fatigue, or stress, it's easy to understand how depression could be mistaken for moodiness. But the symptoms of depression, unlike the symptoms of a temporary mood swing, are chronic and debilitating. They negatively impact an individual's ability to function at work, at school, and in relationships. Individuals suffering from depression often feel numb, apathetic, anxious, disconnected, or uncaring. They also may find it difficult to reveal or discuss these subjective emotional states—a problem that can make diagnosis even more challenging. But the outward signs and symptoms indicating depression are numerous and persistent. Common signs to look for include the following:

- decreased or increased appetite leading to weight change
- insomnia or hypersomnia
- feelings of worthlessness and guilt
- inability to think clearly or concentrate effectively
- indecisiveness
- persistent sad, anxious, or empty moods
- feelings of hopelessness or pessimism
- loss of interest or pleasure in ordinary activities
- decreased energy and fatigue
- restlessness or irritability
- unexplained aches and pains
- thoughts of death or suicide
- anxiety
- loss of friends
- diminished academic performance (However, very bright and perfection-oriented children are often able to maintain good grades in spite of their depression.)

WHAT YOU CAN DO

If untreated, depression may lead to the development of other serious problems. For example, students suffering from depression are more prone to substance abuse, anxiety, delusions, and—the most dire consequence—suicide. These individuals are also more likely to develop speech disorders and learning problems.

In students with any type of depressive disorder, the brain's social operating system is clearly not able to function in the school's social environment. It will have to be strengthened. (Strategies for doing so are discussed in Chapter 2 and in the next section of this chapter.) Do not get sidetracked in pursuing your plan. Here are the essentials:

1. Believe that it will work; know that the brain can and will change with appropriate interventions.

2. Build a team, and make a plan so that every person is on the same page.

3. Focus on building the operating system. This includes building affiliation skills, reward evaluation (see Chapter 2), and the capacity to manage emotional states.

4. Always maintain relationships throughout the process.

5. Be positive and patient. This will take time.

The strategies described in this section can help turn what might at first feel like a hopeless situation into a constructive situation. Don't delay in seeking immediate help. At the very least, consult with the student's parents and with your school psychologist. Once you have done your part to encourage therapeutic intervention, you can help the student in the classroom by providing a positive environment, consistency, and extra emotional support.

Seek Support

All educators should refer any student showing symptoms of potential depression to an appropriate school official, counselor, or psychologist on staff. Teachers should not diagnose or attempt to treat adolescents with suspected depression. Once a diagnosis is given, the referral can trigger the formation of an individualized education plan. Jump in and support the student. Become a part of the team that will support him or her in successfully recovering from depression. Any efforts or steps being taken by parents, teachers, administrators, counselors, physicians, or the student should be communicated to the response team. Make sure that everyone is working together toward the same goals and objectives and that the parties most emotionally involved (e.g., student, parents, teachers) feel supported by the team.

Establish positive routines, and monitor the follow-through. Create high predictability through daily and weekly events that always happen on cue. Start the same way, transition the same way, and end the same way. Add variation only when it is acknowledged as a change.

Focus on positive social actions in the classroom. Acknowledge students' accomplishments, remember their birthdays, and recognize their talents and expert knowledge. By keeping the social status up, you can help all students feel important and remembered.

Incorporate Physical Activity

Movement and exercise can increase production of the "feel good" neurotransmitters that are beneficial in coping with the negative emotions of depression. It is believed that exercise supports healthy levels of serotonin and growth factors, both of which support mood (Chaouloff, 1989; Weicker & Struder, 2001). In addition, brain-derived neurotrophic factor works directly on the serotonin system and can regulate behavior indirectly (Nabkasorn et al., 2006; Stella et al., 2005). Each year, an increasing number of studies suggest that physical activity serves as both a prevention for and treatment of depression.

It continues to astound well-read educators when administrators or policymakers want to reduce or eliminate physical activity. Evidence shows that physical activity is not wasted time; in fact, it is preventative in terms of student anxiety and depression. Incorporate walks, relays, field trips, stretching, aerobics, and classroom energizers into your students' day. Include far more movement, like standing instead of sitting, walking instead of standing, and perching instead of sitting. Although limit open space and time, except in group activities; otherwise it may encourage opportunities for inappropriate impulsivity and movement.

Teach Coping Skills

Teach students to think positively about themselves and their problems as a way to generate new options for their lives. Re-create their train of thought by getting rid of the negative thinking. Encourage the use of relaxation techniques like meditation or yoga. Give students time to explore their emotions through artistic expressions. These activities offer mental and physical relief. Help students recognize that many possible interpretations of any event exist and that they can choose the most empowering one. Illustrate for them the cycle of thinking and feeling that leads to negative outcomes.

Teach Goal Setting

Goal setting can come in many forms. For example, short-term goals may be set for gaining confidence more quickly. Progress reports and debriefings are two types of feedback that are agreeable and useful in this endeavor. Peer feedback, peer editing, cooperative learning, discussion groups, and check-lists are also good methods for learning to set and teach goals.

Provide Nutritional Support

Nutrition contributes to the brain's chemistry, and the chemistry influences mood, cognition, and behavior. Higher levels of serotonin are linked with better attention and mood regulation, which can be influenced by dietary choices. Remind parents about the importance of balanced nutrition when it comes to regulating mood and behavior. A deficiency of many vitamins is associated with adverse psychological symptoms. If students do not get a balanced diet every day, they may need to take nutritional supplements (e.g., multivitamin, multimineral, Omega 3), which have been linked with improved mood. Ask that the parents and/or the school breakfast program offer a balanced breakfast. They should see that students consume complex carbohydrates (such as the whole grains in cereal, pasta, and potatoes) and increase the use of tryptophan, a calming agent found in foods such as avocadoes, milk, and turkey. Quality proteins (e.g., lean meats, yogurt, nuts, eggs) support better mental focus and memory. It is also important to be sure to remove allergens from the diet of a student who has food allergies.

Encourage Lifestyle Changes

Encourage students with depression to change their routine. Suggest that they limit watching television and surfing the Internet and instead join groups, clubs, or teams with a positive mission, one that aims to help something or someone outside of themselves (e.g., the environment, the elderly, the less fortunate). If this does not interest them, then provide a variety of stimulating learning activities to challenge their minds and start thinking in new ways. These activities should not create any sort of academic stress, though. Think of them more as physical activities for the mind.

REVISITING THE STUDENT

"Michelle," one of the learners introduced in the pretest at the front of the book, is the student who fits the profile for depression. Like the others, Michelle is unique—she exhibits a pattern of symptoms that are associated with a specific disorder. However, some of these symptoms can be observed in other conditions as well. This is why you want to look for patterns, rather than isolated behaviors. To help you remember what's important in assessing students with depression, take a moment, relax, and focus on the photo, the symptoms, and the key points of this chapter.

Symptoms

- Decrease in energy
- Change in appetite and subsequent weight loss or gain
- Feelings of worthlessness and guilt
- Inability to think clearly or concentrate; indecisiveness
- Angry, sometimes suicidal imaginings
- Persistent sad, anxious, or empty mood
- Feelings of hopelessness; pessimism
- Loss of interest or pleasure in ordinary activities or hobbies
- Restlessness, irritability, unexplained aches and pains
- Unusual loss of friends; reduction in academic performance

SUPPLEMENTAL RESOURCES

Books

The Bipolar Child, by Janice Papolos

Body Blues, by Laura Weeldreyer

Coping With Teen Suicide, by James Murphy

Darkness Visible, by William Styron

How to Cope with Depression, by Raymond DePaulo

The Life of a Bipolar Child, by Trudy Carlson

Major Depression: The Forgotten Illness, by Paul A. Kettl, MD

Teen Depression, by Lisa Wolf

The Unquiet Mind, by Kay Redfield Jamison

Ups and Downs: How to Beat the Blues, by Susan Klebanoff

Web sites

Continuing Medical Education: www.cmellc.com

Depression.com: www.depression.com

Dr. Ivan's Depression Central: www.psycom.net/depression.central.html

MedLine Plus: www.nlm.nih.gov/medlineplus/depression.html

Teen Health From Nemours:
www.kidshealth.org/teen/your_mind/mental_health/depression.html

8

The Isolated Learner

Pervasive Developmental Disorders

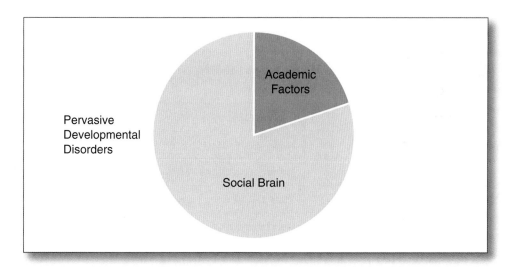

Years ago, parents with children who were withdrawn dismissed them as unsociable. They were a lonely lot and thought of as "different." Today, we know differently. Autism and Asperger syndrome are the two pervasive developmental disorders (PDD) that receive the majority of media coverage and attention. However, PDD also covers Rett syndrome, childhood disintegrative disorder, and PDD-NOS (not otherwise specified).

There is still tremendous controversy about what causes PDD. But the good news is that most with a PDD can be helped. This chapter focuses mostly on autism and Asperger syndrome (two different but related disorders) since we see these students the most in our schools.

Most of the PDDs are rare; the most common one is Asperger syndrome (see Table 8.1). Named after Hans Asperger, an Austrian psychiatrist and pediatrician, the disorder was recognized in the fourth edition of the American Psychiatric Association's *Diagnostic and Statistical Manual of Mental Disorders* in 1994. In people with this disorder, language may develop normally, IQ is generally average or above, and they typically have a narrow area of interests. Many are highly functioning and exhibit sensory issues as well as impaired socialization. Many view someone with Asperger syndrome as having a difference rather than a disability. Some experts use the Autism Diagnostic Interview-Revised semistructured parent interview for diagnosis, while others use the Autism Diagnostic Observation Schedule, a conversation and play-based interview for use with children.

Autism is not a new disorder. In fact, in 1911 Swiss psychiatrist Eugen Bleuler, who was describing adult schizophrenia, first used the word *autism* (from the Greek word for *self*). Then Leo Kanner of Johns Hopkins University described autism as it is known today (Stotz-Ingenlath, 2000). Autism is a high-variable developmental and spectrum disorder. It is characterized by an impaired immune system, lack of *theory of mind* (the ability

Table 8.1   Strengths and Challenges of a Student With Asperger Syndrome

Strengths	Challenges
Honest	Making friends
Determined	Managing feelings
An expert	Taking advice
Kind	Handwriting
Speaks his or her mind	Knowing when someone is thinking
Enjoys solitude	Being teased or bullied
Perfectionist	Showing as much affection as others expect
Reliable friend	Switching tasks
Good at art	Changing environments
Liked by adults	Varying approaches and strategies

to intuit what another is thinking, to "walk in their shoes"), and persever-
ative behaviors. Likely causes are a combination of genetic predispositions
with one or more environmental triggers. It is not actually a disease, but a
cluster of behaviors (or syndrome).

Diagnosis for autism can be made as early as 12 to 18 months. Accurate
diagnosis of Asperger syndrome often must wait until 2 to 5 years of age
(Pennington, James, McNally, Pay, & McConachie, 2009) because the symptoms are often emergent and milder. A variety of screening tests are available, including the Modified Checklist for Autism in Toddlers, Autism
Spectrum Screening Questionnaire, Australian Scale for Asperger's
Syndrome, and the Childhood Asperger Syndrome Test (Scahill, 2005).

At each stage of development—from prenatal well into early childhood—
there is an additional window of vulnerability that can increase the
symptoms of autism. These are the four stages of vulnerability and the
dominant factors:

- genes (chromosomes 6 and 17)
- in utero (hormones and toxins may exacerbate at this age)
- 0–36 months old (impaired immune system)
- 3–8 years old (behavioral changes may arise from gene expression)

By the age of 12 months, signs of autism might be observed. Characteristics
of those with autism vary widely, but common early signs include
the following:

- nontypical eye contact, lack of visual tracking, disengagement of
  visual attention
- prolonged latency to disengage visual attention
- alternating pattern of extreme passivity and extreme distress
  reactions
- tendency to fixate on particular objects in the environment
- decreased expression of positive affect
- delayed expressive and receptive language
- lack of orienting to name
- lack of imitation, social smiling, social interest
- lack of affect and sensory-oriented behaviors

It is important to understand that there are many types of autism.
Classic autism is the most severe and the most commonly understood of the
autism spectrum disorders. People with classic autism commonly have a
great deal of trouble interacting with others, strong sensory issues, health
problems, and developmental delays. About 25 to 30 percent also have
seizures (Pavone et al., 2004). Complex autism is exhibited in individuals for
whom there is evidence of abnormal early embryonic development, with
either differences in physical appearance or small head size. Individuals

with this type of autism tend to have lower IQs, more seizures, more abnormal EEGs, and more brain MRI differences. Interventions have an uneven track record.

IMPACT

The impact of these disorders has obviously raised concern among modern parents, scientists, and journalists seeking to unearth some answers. Over the past 30 years, the number of those diagnosed with autism has skyrocketed, and many have asked if this is a false epidemic. Roy Richard Grinker, a professor of anthropology at George Washington University who has studied perceptions of autism, has a personal as well as professional interest in the subject: his daughter was diagnosed with the developmental disorder at the age of 2. Dr. Grinker argues that the definitions have broadened over the years and that there has been a "relabeling" from other diagnoses. The categorization of what is developmentally different is wider than in years past, and kids once labeled as having one particular disorder are now being reassigned to a different category, often PDD. Additionally, Grinker argues, there are financial incentives for schools and parents to identify children, enabling additional resources to be brought to the table. But others argue that it was underdiagnosed before and we are just now catching up.

Demographics

Autism affects more boys than girls by a ratio of 4:1, and Asperger syndrome continues to be the most common of PDDs. It occurs in about 1 in 166 children, or 7 per 1,000 that have a PDD (Pereira et al., 2007). The rigorous Brick Township (New Jersey) study found that the prevalence rate for all PDD was 6.70 cases per 1,000 children (Bertrand et al., 2001). Many believe that these disorders show up much more in certain cultures, which suggests a genetic link. Compare the earlier U.S. numbers to the findings in Beijing, China, where the prevalence rate is 0.80 per 1,000 children (Liu et al., 2005). In a U.S. school with 500 children, you might expect 2 to 4 kids to have PDD. The number of cases is rising, but so are the capacity and tools for diagnosis.

Likely Causes

There is no single, verified cause of PDD. Various causes have been examined, including multiple brain-body dysfunctions, genetic influences, and gene expression. And environmental toxins exacerbate these causes, leading to an altered theory of mind with different brain structures and functional capacity.

Autism is likely not one but multiple dysfunctions with multiple causes. The most likely cause of the cluster of symptoms stems from genetic and nonspecific environmentally responsive genes (i.e., gene expressions that are probably associated with large-scale systemic changes; Herbert et al., 2006). Given the multitude of factors possibly attributing to PDD, the worst-case scenario occurs when all four areas—genetic susceptibility, exposure in utero, compromised immune system, and aberrant gene expression from environmental factors—converge in an individual.

When individuals with autism grow up, the majority of them do not have children, which means that if autism were 100 percent genetic, the incidence of the presumed genes in the population would decrease with time because of childless autistic adults. But the numbers are rising, so there are clearly other components at play (Hainsworth, 2006). There are spontaneous genetic mutations that have stronger links to autism and Asperger syndrome (Stone, McMahon, Yoder, & Walden, 2007) than previously recognized. But it's a two-way street as far as how genes and environment interact to shape behavior. Gene expression is the capacity to respond to acute or chronic environmental input. Through mRNA, a gene's proteins are translated and activated to influence the structures and functions of a cell, which is the basis for cellular differentiation versatility and cellular adaptability (Rossi, 2002).

Keep in mind that we are still in the early days of understanding these brain and body differences. Autism and Asperger syndrome are complex. There are multiple breakdowns in the mind and body, and as of today there is no one treatment for all of them at once. But there are effective treatments for each separately.

Vaccine Theory

All vaccines temporarily create immune system responses. Receiving more vaccines in less time increases the risk of temporarily weakening the immune system, but strengthens it for the long haul. The mercury in most vaccines has been removed, though a small percentage of uncommon vaccines still contain thimerosal, a mercury-containing compound used as a preservative in the serums (U.S. Food and Drug Administration, n.d.). Scientists at the U.S. Food and Drug Administration and elsewhere continue researching the theory that vaccines may have a triggering effect on PDD. Even though mercury has been removed from most vaccines, there has been no dramatic drop in cases of autism, suggesting that the problem may be more complex.

Biochemistry and Hormone Theory

Hormone imbalances may contribute to different brain behaviors. Varied levels of chemicals such as testosterone, serotonin, and oxytocin in the mother can affect a newborn's socialization capacity, gender, and learning capacity (Knickmeyer, Baron-Cohen, Raggatt, & Taylor, 2005). Current research also shows that altering brain chemistry can help those with autism. For example, Buspirone, a pharmaceutical used to treat generalized anxiety disorder, may help. And serotonin agonists may be helpful for children with autism who are under the age of 5 (Chugani, Juhász, Behen, Ondersma, & Muzik 2007).

Among many roles, oxytocin is involved in social recognition, social acceptance, lowering fear and bonding, and formation of trust. It also improves the ability to recognize emotions like happiness and anger in people's tone of voice, something those with autism struggle with. In one study, a single infusion produced improvements that lasted two weeks: when given oxytocin, the amygdala activity lowered, indicating that the fear response declined with injections and suggesting that oxytocin medicates social fear and trust (Passik & Kirsch, 2006).

Brain Areas Involved

Many children with autism have severe brain dysfunction, and one-third will develop epilepsy by adulthood (Steffenburg, 1991). In terms of difference in brain functioning for individuals with PDD, like intelligence, their brain size varies widely. Brain areas in question include the amygdala, caudate nuclei, cerebellum, overall brain mass, and left inferior frontal gyrus (Schaefer, Mendelsohn, & Professional Practice and Guidelines Committee, 2008; see Figure 8.1).

Figure 8.1   Brain Areas and Functions Affected by PDD

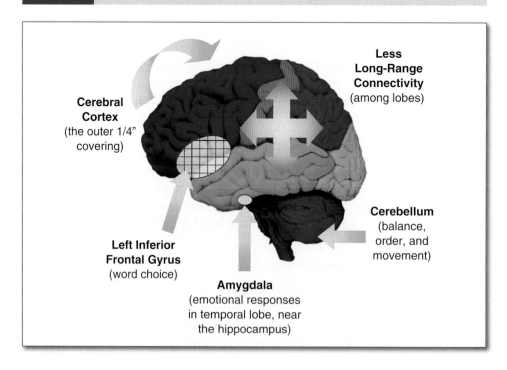

Kids with Asperger syndrome often find it very stressful to meet new people. Figure 8.2 offers a side-by-side comparison of the stimulus responses of a typical child and a child with autism upon one of these first encounters. Their brain interprets eye contact as being threatening and it prompts raised cortisol levels.

Mirror Neurons

Mirror neurons, which have been discovered in animals and humans, are goal oriented and help the brain identify and rehearse potential learning. They are special brain cells that fire both when one performs an action and when one observes the same action performed by another. Thus, the neuron "mirrors" the behavior of another, as though the observer were itself performing the action. Located in the premotor cortex and the inferior parietal cortex, these may be the source of empathy and imitation learning. Mimicking is a trait of healthy primates and is needed in order to learn, so a defective mirror neuron system may be linked to autism.

Cortal Connectivity

The autistic brain has location-specific overconnectivity, but it also has large-scale underconnectivity. It is a highly compartmentalized brain, whereas the traditionally gifted tend to have a highly connected brain (Singh & O'Boyle, 2004).

Figure 8.2 How the Body Responds in Typical Children Versus Those With PDD When Meeting Others

Typical

1 Visual information relayed to amygdala.
2 No rise in activation and heart rate continues normally.
3 Eye contact and healthy communication continues.

PDD

1 Visual information relayed to amygdala.
2 Fast rise in heart rate activation and stress levels elevate.
3 Eye contact is averted and communication is difficult.

Recognizable Symptoms

While environmental and genetic factors might play into PDD, there is some danger in making generalizations on this topic. Everyone is unique, and you cannot say, "All of those with Asperger syndrome do this or that," because PDD symptoms vary widely in type and severity. For example, autism symptoms include impairment in social interaction, a fixation on inanimate objects, repetitive behaviors, the inability to communicate normally, and resistance to changes in daily routine. Many of these are aligned with the five common symptoms for those with PDD (see Figure 8.3).

Specific symptoms of PDD may also include

- nontypical eye contact, lack of visual tracking, disengagement of visual attention
- prolonged latency to disengage visual attention
- alternating pattern of extreme passivity and extreme distress reactions
- tendency to fixate on particular objects in the environment
- decreased expression of positive affect
- delayed expressive and receptive language
- lack of orienting to name
- lack of imitation, social smiling, social interest
- lack of affect and sensory-oriented behaviors

Let's explore each characteristic a little further.

Figure 8.3   Five Characteristic Symptoms of PDD

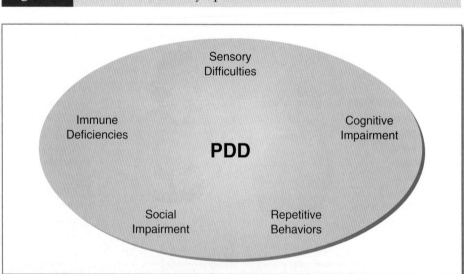

Sensory Difficulties

Students with PDD inhabit a world where their sensory system seems to hold them captive to a chaotic and overwhelming world of stress. The autistic brain does not filter incoming signals well. Instead of hearing too little, a person with autism may hear too much and be unable to filter out the noise or prioritize. Unexpected touches, sounds, or sights can be startling and stressful (Grossberg & Seidman, 2006).

Repetitive Behaviors

Students with autism often display various forms of hand and arm flapping. Sensory issues may be correlated with the repetitive behaviors. There may be obsessive routine and a preoccupation with a particular subject of interest. This is stimulus-driven behavior triggered by only the most salient, stressful feature of the environment (Ridley, 1994). This tendency, known as perseveration, can display in those with Asperger syndrome as fixated, repetitive task-driven behavior.

Cognitive Impairment

Cognitively, students with PDD have a wide range of ability and intelligence. They have poor ability at generalizations, instead being literal in their interpretations. They also like to focus on a single idea rather than multiple ideas, since they prefer unambiguous thinking. Additionally, they have a tendency to compartmentalize and prefer numbers, simple texts, and photos (Cherkassky, Kana, Keller, & Just, 2006).

Those with PDD do not realize that others may have different thoughts, plans, and perspectives than their own. This theory has been validated, even with the recent discovery of mirror neurons (Southgate & Hamilton, 2008).

Social Impairment (Theory of Mind)

When engaged in social situations, students with autism have inappropriate emotional responsiveness. Looking someone in the eye is hard for them since it seems threatening. And when they do focus on a face, they pay attention to irrelevant features. Connecting with people is rather difficult since they are unable to express their emotions in typical ways (Elgar & Campbell, 2001). Typically they have little or no clue what another is thinking about, even when this is quite clear to others, which puts them at a tremendous disadvantage in social interactions where prediction and reciprocity are critical for friendships.

Immune Deficiencies

A compromised immune system starts in utero and/or is activated by environmental triggers. For example, a child may have a genetic predisposition to a PDD, and with exposure to certain environmental triggers the disorder may reveal itself. These triggers might include childhood vaccinations, exposure to preservatives in vaccines, daily exposure to toxins of unregulated agents, and biochemical imbalances with thromboxane (an indicator of platelet activity) and prostacyclin (an indicator of constricting endothelial cells; Yao, Walsh, McGinnis, & Pratico, 2006).

WHAT YOU CAN DO

As of yet, there are no magic cures for every case of PDD. There are countless "miracle" stories of those who have been successfully treated, but from individual cases it's hard to generalize the treatment to all cases. Let's start with the basics:

- The five characteristic symptoms of PDD are repetitive behaviors, immune deficiencies, sensory difficulties, social impairment, and cognitive impairment.
- Every student with any PDD is unique, and generalizations can be misleading.
- Begin with a solid and detailed inventory of the areas you want to strengthen.
- Focus your work on the life skills that will support independence and inclusion.
- Both the social and academic operating systems need upgrades.
- Never give up.

It is clear in students with PDD that the brain's social operating system is not up to the task of the school's social environment. It will have to be strengthened. (Strategies for doing so are discussed in Chapter 2 and in the next section of this chapter.) Do not get sidetracked in pursuing your plan. Here are the essentials:

1. Believe that it will work; know that the brain can and will change with appropriate interventions.

2. Build a team, and make a plan so that every person is on the same page.

3. Focus on building the operating system, specifically by managing emotional states and developing theory of mind.

4. Always maintain relationships throughout the process.

5. Be positive and patient. This will take time.

The strategies described in the following section can help turn what might at first feel like a hopeless situation into a constructive situation:

Provide an environment that ensures fairness and sameness. For example, establish predictable routines by continually using the same schedule and seating environments. Focus on keeping the environmental stressors low, and eliminate all teasing or bullying. Allow students to flourish in their own time. Do not push eye contact. Children with autism may avoid eye contact because it is perceived as stressful or even threatening.

The brain is designed to respond to environmental input. Intensive early intervention studies indicate that by age 5 over 50 percent of children with Asperger syndrome overcome language and social skill deficits enough to participate with their families, schools, and communities. All kids can improve to a degree. It just depends on the severity of the autism and the resources brought to the table (Sallows & Graupner, 2005).

Utilize the Sea of Hope intervention method (see Chapter 1) when adapting teaching styles to serve students with PDD. These intervention techniques—skill building, enrichment, and accommodations—must be customized and pieced together. Skill building needs to be the focus for 30 to 90 minutes, four to six times a week, with relevant, high-interest techniques. The initial skill-development needs should be addressed through individual or microgroup instruction, not in large classes. Individual teaching episodes are used to establish basic language, social, and cognitive skills. As each of the routines is learned independently, the one-on-one instruction and prompting is reduced.

When there is a lack of joint attention, it means that the intervention is needed to attract and sustain the child's attention. Social exchanges need deliberate planning and ongoing structuring by the teacher.

Develop Intervention Techniques

When it comes to assisting children with PDD, you can work on a multitude of skill-building areas such as behavior, sensory retaining, communication skills, social skills, facial recognition, and vocabulary. These children need to be directly taught various social skills. They will not pick these up from others. Use social stories, social scripts, storyboarding, role-playing, comic strip conversations, individualized social rule cards, and peer partners/buddies. When seeking to build social skills, model how to initiate and maintain appropriate social interactions (e.g., on the playground they might ask, "Wanna play ball?").

Create a successful conversation by taking turns asking questions; this develops reciprocal communication skills. Teach students how to ask other people questions related to topics initiated by them. In simple conversations, tell them how long to talk. To break down the communication patterns, start a conversation by calling a person by his or her name to gain the personalized attention. Tone of voice, personal space, vocal volume, body orientation, and facial expressions are important to establishing a good conversation.

Model how to start and end a conversation because these are great examples of skills that are important in establishing and maintaining friendships. Review this checklist to help students with Asperger syndrome flourish in conversations:

- knowing when to start and stop
- assessing the degree of reciprocity
- staying on track
- making affirming/confirming statements
- knowing how to repair conversations
- making relevant statements
- knowing when and how to interrupt
- being aware of body language, gestures, and eye contact

In skill building, retention relies on students having the following:

- focused attention
- repetition over time
- buy-in (a sense of hope and optimism)
- good nutrition
- feedback (both positive and negative)
- quality sleep
- practice of 30 to 90 minutes a day, three to six times a week (Huttenlocher, Vasilyeva, Cymerman, & Levine, 2002)

Anything less than all of these variables will reduce the brain's capacity to make rapid neurological change. The interventions must be comprehensive and intensive. Intensity means ongoing and relentless functional, developmentally relevant, and high-interest opportunities.

Attunement, the quality of time spent on an intervention, is essential to working with these students. Use games, conversations, activities, manners, faces, and affection displays to enrich and encourage them to open up. These emotional-social development activities are essential for many reasons. Occasionally, additional problems may exacerbate the lack of social skills. For example, abuse, neglect, or misattunement (socially reciprocal bonding games) may lead to overpruning of synapses in the right prefrontal cortex, causing an inability to modulate emotions. Kids with an autistic spectrum disorder need coherent, purposeful social skill building.

Incorporate Behavior Modification

The most successful programs for behavior modification are multi-pronged. You need to start these as early as possible. They require spending substantial floor time (e.g., patty-cake, hide-and-seek, mirroring games) with the child. Also be sure to gain 100 percent support from the caregivers, which includes having them pay particular attention to their child's nutritional intake. This will need to continue for months in order for the child to modify and adapt the behaviors.

Two verbal-behavior programs are highly effective: Natural Environment Teaching (NET) and Pivotal Response Training (PRT). NET stimulates and engages, but the child's responses should be related to what's valuable to him or her at that moment. Research suggests avoiding isolating strategies. In fact, the more you create a motivating social environment, the quicker kids with autism can improve.

PRT is a behavioral treatment intervention based on the principles of applied behavior analysis. Researchers have identified two pivotal behaviors that affect a wide range of behaviors in children with autism: motivation and responsivity to multiple cues (Koegel, Bimbela, & Schriebman, 1996).

Facilitate Adaptability to Change

Keeping stress low is important for students with PDD. They may feel an utter lack of control in the environment, prompting them to become rather stressed. To keep such stressful situations under control, tell these students predictions of upcoming events so that they can gain a little confidence and control. Other important ways to keep the stress level low include the following:

1. Teach coping skills to help students deal with changes (talk them through tough situations and model appropriate responses).

2. Offer assurances of safety (let them know what's coming up, who will be there to help out, and what the safety net of support is).

3. Encourage them to use tools for self-control (e.g., taking a deep breath, counting to 10, holding on to comforting objects).

4. Provide likely scenarios of any changes (e.g., "In a moment, we'll be going into another room. It will have several adults seated in it. It will be safe for us. We'll walk in and sit down.").

Provide Physical Education

Many students with PDD are clumsy and not confident in their gross motor skills. They often lack coordination, have severe balance problems, and have difficulty with graphology skills. Do not ask them to perform physical activities that might embarrass them. Rather than asking them to perform in competitive team sports, offer simple physical activities such as partnered walks, free play, cycling, running, or swimming. This outlet helps reduce stress and may promote the production of vital chemicals and processes in the brain.

Use Visual Strategies

Teaching them to see the big picture first helps students with PDD navigate the visual task. These students often have poor visual recall, faulty spatial perceptions, difficulty with executive functioning, and problems with spatial relations. Present wholes first (rather than specific parts). Use tactile arts to encourage building and arranging items because this helps them gain control.

When setting up and organizing a classroom, hang poster visuals on the walls. Color coding helps provide space-based cues for what to do when and where. Visual schedules with objects, flow charts, photos, and symbols help students with PDD build a simple system and visual syntax. The visual language should include the written word, with symbols or photos to help pair abstractions with those words. Use emotion cards (i.e., artistic renderings of emotional faces and their paired emotions) as a means of expression.

Use Tactile-Kinesthetic Strategies

Provide students with PDD with tools and devices that allow them to destress and gain control of the environment. Such devices include music sticks, exercise balls, pillows, Koosh balls, swings, rocker boards, and chin-up bars to suspend from. These allow outlets for students' physical energy, which in turn will help their brains stabilize.

Use Communication Strategies

Students with PDD often lack the ability to comprehend nonverbal communication, have difficulty adjusting to transitions and novel situations, and show deficits in social judgment and social interaction. It is important to model the desired behavior instead of just saying it. The predictability of the rules interests them, in terms of sequencing (e.g., "If you do this, then you can do that.").

Offer students the Picture Exchange Communication System (PECS), whereby you ask them to hand a picture to an adult to communicate what they want. The adult speaks the word to reinforce it. Other important communicative skill programs include responsivity education for parents and Prelinguistic Milieu Teaching (PMT). This program teaches communication within the context of play and is better for kids who have greater language strengths.

Note that for increasing joint attention skills, PECS is superior to PMT for children who have very little joint attention to begin with. Conversely, PMT is better than PECS for children who originally had more joint attention skills. For increasing the use of spoken language, PECS is superior to PMT. Language and communication skills increase for children receiving both types of interventions (Yücel et al., 2007).

Your individualized education plan objectives should focus on speech and language and also include development of social skills, expressive verbal language, a functional symbolic communication system, increased engagement and flexibility in tasks and play, fine and gross motor skills, cognitive skills, reduction in problem behaviors, and independent organizational skills.

Build the Social Brain

Many strategic paths can strengthen the parts of the social brain's operating system that can build functionality and inclusion for students with PDD. A software program called Let's Face It may be helpful in building facial recognition skills.

The web simulation Second Life allows kids to pick a virtual human (avatar) that moves through life and must interact with others. This helps introduce the demands of social experiences. Brains are designed to change. They adapt to experience, for better or worse. Students with PDD can improve. How much improvement depends on the how well the Sea of Hope is implemented and whether students' brains are continually renewed with information.

Use Cognitive Tools

Support students with PDD through the use of well-rounded cognitive tools. Teach with concrete images and tools, rather than temporal or abstract information (e.g., talking through directions too much). Avoid repeating things three times; rather, improve comprehension with visual tools (e.g., books, writing the page numbers on the board).

Set Goals

Providing students with PDD with goals is important to their success. The initial primary goal of education is to teach personal independence and social responsibility (with reduction of disruptive behavioral problems). Secondarily, priorities should include functional spontaneous communication, social instruction, cognitive development, play skills, and behavior. Overall, progress toward achieving students' goals should be monitored frequently and adjusted accordingly.

Can Autism Be Cured?

The answer to this question is: not usually. However, there are many individual cases of miracles and unexpected success in this field. Remember that each person is unique. The human brain is designed to adapt to change, so by changing the environment you can change the brain. How much each brain will change depends on a host of factors, some known and some unknown. At this time, here are the factors we know are critical:

- Starting earlier is better than starting later in life.
- Doing something is better than doing nothing.
- It will take more time and resources than you think.
- High-quality nutrition never hurts and often helps.
- Certain agonist drugs (those that may raise serotonin and oxytocin) can help students' progress.
- Everything plays off of other things—synergy matters.
- It is important to work on multiple things each week (e.g., nutrition, movement, skills).
- Progress does not happen in a straight line—expect temporary setbacks.

The take-home message here is one of hope. Be the beacon of hope that helps students continually rebuild the body and brain. If you are doing the right things, and if you are relentless in your efforts, the brain will change. Resistance to change is futile.

REVISITING THE STUDENT

"Robert," one of the learners introduced in the pretest at the front of the book, is the student who fits the profile for PDD. Like the others, Robert is unique—he exhibits a pattern of symptoms that are associated with a specific disorder. However, some of these symptoms can be observed in other conditions as well. This is why you want to look for patterns, rather than isolated behaviors. To help you remember what's important in assessing students with PDD, take a moment, relax, and focus on the photo, the symptoms, and the key points of this chapter.

Symptoms

- Stays to himself
- Often gets stuck and repeats behaviors
- Seems obsessed with details
- Dislikes changes of routines or surprises
- Makes little or no eye contact
- Gets sick more often than others
- Misses the big picture
- Shows fascination over apparent trivia

SUPPLEMENTAL RESOURCES

Books

1001 Great Ideas for Teaching and Raising Children With Autism Spectrum Disorders, by Veronica Zysk and Ellen Notbohm

Children With Starving Brains: A Medical Treatment Guide for Autism Spectrum Disorder, by Jaquelyn McCandless

Guide to Scientific Nutrition for Autism, by Kirkman Laboratories

The Kid-Friendly ADHD and Autism Cookbook: The Ultimate Guide to the Gluten-Free, Casein-Free Diet, by Pamela Compart and Dana Laake

Nobody Nowhere: The Extraordinary Autobiography of an Autistic, by Donna Williams

Ten Things Every Child With Autism Wishes You Knew, by Ellen Notbohm

Thinking in Pictures, by Temple Grandin

Understanding Nonverbal Learning Disabilities: A Common-Sense Guide for Parents and Professionals, by Maggie Mamen

Unstrange Minds: Remapping the World of Autism, by Roy Roger Grinker

The Unwritten Rules of Social Relationships: Decoding Social Mysteries Through the Unique Perspectives of Autism, by Temple Grandin and Sean Barron

Web sites

Abilitations: www.abilitations.com

Autism Watch: www.autism-watch.org

Autism Web, Applied Behavior Analysis and Verbal Behavior: www.autismweb.com/aba.htm

9

The Challenged Learner

Learning Delayed

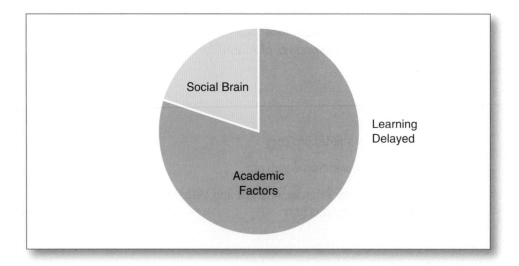

We've all known a student who seemed a step behind his or her peers. Years ago this was the kid who was teased, taunted, and even ridiculed. Today, we know it's more likely that his or her brain may have learning delays. *Learning delayed* (LD), or delayed development, is a term used to describe a child's failure to make the usual developmental milestones typical of his or her age. There is not one, but multiple such disorders. Kids with delays struggle with reading, writing, math, speech, language, memory, and other basic skills. Overall, the nationwide average is that 5 to 8 percent of all children have some sort of learning delay, including subtypes. This means that at least 5 out of every 100 kids at school will likely fall within this category.

The term LD is used euphemistically for borderline to mild mental retardation. However, because of the enormous plasticity of the young human brain, many children who are "delayed" catch up later. Of course, many don't catch up, and while some functions (e.g., thinking, motor skills, emotional development) may be preserved, other areas may be impaired.

A number of potential factors contribute to delayed development and LD, including history of schizophrenia, genetic problems, brain injuries, malnutrition, fetal alcohol exposure, autism, impoverished environments, neglect, and inadequate care. One or more of the following factors, as they are generically called, commonly cause brain injuries or brain insults:

- blows to the head (e.g., falls, being hit by objects, domestic abuse)
- environmental exposure to toxins (e.g., metals, chemicals, air pollution)
- sports or car accidents
- accidents on children's recreational vehicles (e.g., bicycle, skateboard, sled, skates)
- prenatal exposure to drugs and toxins (e.g., tobacco, narcotics, alcohol)
- concussion-prone sports (e.g., football, soccer, baseball, hockey)
- falls or unprotected impact (e.g., falling down stairs or from a bunk bed, hit by door, kicked by horse)
- difficult births and maternal infection

In spite of continued affluence in developed countries, contributing factors such as poverty, broken families, violence, and inadequate parenting skills are still prevalent. These conditions, combined with the role of genetics, contribute to the problems that affect millions of children in our schools. There is significant potential for the developing fetus and the developing child to be impacted by unhealthy conditions. Considering the magnitude of this problem, having even a single healthy student in the classroom could be considered miraculous. Such students typically have been nurtured in a nuclear family, have had no exposure to toxins, and have developed strong emotional and social skills. Unfortunately, however, these students are not the norm.

An accurate LD diagnosis relies on careful descriptions of a child's communicative strengths and weaknesses with observation and testing. The impairment is summarized by the ability to take multiple pieces of information and pull them together to form a single, integrated picture or pattern. That is why students with LD can function well at younger ages yet become overwhelmed as they get older. The statistically unusual event is the discrepancy between different intellectual skills within the same brain.

IMPACT

The impact of delayed learning on schools is growing. Presently, the trend is to embrace all learners, even those with significant developmental challenges, in mainstream classrooms. One challenge is that most regular education teachers are not trained to deal with these challenged students, a factor that adds to the problems of the already stressed-out staff. Consider these significant impacts: Many challenged students fall through the cracks, minimal (if any) learning occurs, and then they are passed on to the next grade level where the injustice is repeated. Teachers grow increasingly frustrated and overwhelmed, resulting in widespread hopelessness and resignation. With the right tools and resources, teachers can make a dramatic difference. Otherwise, the students have little chance.

Demographics

As with other disorders, there is a tremendous amount of comorbidity with other problems. For example, delayed development/LD is often present in families in which there is domestic abuse, maternal smoking, or alcohol/drug abuse—all of which can lead to a host of other problems in children.

Commentary

LD constitutes a moderate to high level of challenge to the classroom teacher. You can contribute to this learner's success, but you will need support from others—notably the parents and learning specialists.

Likely Causes

As described previously, many dominating factors cause or contribute to LD, including neonatal seizures, a poor learning environment (due to a parent's learning disability), developmental trauma (e.g., abuse, isolation, neglect during infancy), environmental toxins (e.g., cadmium, lead, mercury), chemotherapy for childhood cancer, central nervous system infections, chronic illnesses (e.g., diabetes, asthma), and poor nutrition. Although every one of these problems deserves attention, another problem is the most pervasive: fetal alcohol syndrome (FAS). Much of what we can learn from it also relates to the other conditions that cause developmental and learning delays. In other words, FAS symptoms and the suggested treatments form a good guideline for all of the contributing factors of these delays.

Fetal Alcohol Syndrome

Alcohol is the most potent toxin to an unborn child's brain. Ethanol exceeds the toxic effects of maternal ingestion of cocaine or heroin. It stunts the growth of the brain and new neuron production during pregnancy. Studies suggest that FAS is presently the single most prevalent cause of mental retardation and developmental and learning delays in the United States. Someone with FAS might demonstrate a very uneven performance, impaired speech and language, and facial abnormalities. However, other significant health implications are associated with FAS as well. It is believed that FAS may increase the risk of childhood leukemia, fetal hypoxia, oral clefts, and respiratory tract infections. It is also correlated with hyperactivity, impulsivity, and learning disorders.

Babies with FAS are typically characterized by a smaller head, smaller brain, and some mental retardation or LD. Although the research on FAS indicates that even light drinking in pregnancy (especially during the most critical times of fetal development) can lead to FAS effects, binge drinking while pregnant is almost certain to impact the baby's health. A sudden surge of alcohol, even during a single evening celebration, can have devastating effects. It appears that timing is a factor. The months (not days!) before conception and the subsequent eight weeks following conception (when a mother is least likely to know she's pregnant) appear to be the most critical periods. It is difficult to estimate the quantity of alcohol that poses a risk since there is such a wide variance among women in their ability to metabolize alcohol, so most healthcare professionals recommend that pregnant women abstain during pregnancy.

In spite of these findings and the health warnings on all alcoholic beverage containers, data suggest that consumption of alcoholic beverages may be increasing among pregnant women. Binge drinking (even one episode) poses more profound risk, and drinking during the last trimester can destroy large groups of neurons. Typically, women who consume alcohol during pregnancy also exhibit other risk factors, such as a lack of prenatal care, exposure to domestic abuse, and drug use.

FAS has long-term consequences for both the individual and society. A predictable, long-term progression of the disorder into adulthood challenges communities as they struggle to respond to the maladaptive behaviors of the adult FAS victim. This serious condition is, in fact, one of the leading causes of birth defects.

Prenatal Drug Exposure

Some pregnant women use over-the-counter medications that are contraindicated during pregnancy. Use of such drugs presents a risk to the unborn child. Most physicians urge pregnant women to abstain from alcohol, but the message that other drugs (including prescription and over-the-counter medications) are also dangerous needs to be articulated.

Infants exposed to cocaine show signs of toxicity similar to the abnormalities that result from in utero exposure to crack, heroin, tobacco, and amphetamines. All pose significant health risks. The degree of disability varies widely depending on the degree of exposure, the timing of it, the comorbidity factors, and the postnatal living environment. Fetuses occasionally exposed to light doses of cocaine during the third trimester may achieve normalcy, provided they are raised in a loving and nurturing home and are exposed to no other known toxic factors. However, they remain at higher risk for other problems should they experience any complicating variables.

While early studies failed to find any correlation between maternal crack use and the baby's IQ, the tests used evaluated standard intelligence measures only. More recently, studies have indicated that cocaine may damage areas of the brain that regulate arousal, attention, and emotions. These aspects of intelligence, though not measured in standard IQ tests, indeed impact a child's ability to function successfully in the world.

Malnutrition

Some studies have shown that infants in developing countries who received supplemental formula (the international standard formulation) had significantly more intentional solutions to problems when compared to a nonsupplemented sample of the population. Higher problem-solving scores in infancy are related to higher childhood IQ scores; thus, good nutrition may enhance childhood intelligence.

In malnourished children there is a high prevalence of "stunting"—an indication of poverty, social deprivation, disease, and resulting cognitive impairment; however, the problem extends beyond the conditions of poverty. All socioeconomic classes witness the problem. It is not atypical, for example, for a middle-class child's diet to contain too much sugar, starch, and junk food, and not enough nutrients and protein. In fact, more children in America are malnourished than in Angola, Zimbabwe, Cambodia, Haiti, and El Salvador combined.

Iron deficiency is the single most common nutritional disorder worldwide and the cause of anemia during infancy, childhood, and pregnancy. Anemia is linked to short attention span, disruptive behaviors, and impaired memory. It is prevalent in most of the developing world as well as in industrialized nations.

Kwashiorkor syndrome, characterized by retarded growth, changes in skin and hair pigment, edema, and pathologic changes in the liver (including fatty infiltration, necrosis, and fibrosis), is a condition produced by severe protein deficiency. Although first reported in Africa, Kwashiorkor syndrome is now known throughout the world. Other variations of protein deficiencies, including those seen in some vegans, exist as well. Protein deficiencies have been linked to aggressive behaviors.

Maternal Tobacco Use

Smoking cigarettes during pregnancy puts the fetus at risk for miscarriage, possible death, and low birth weight. The most common disability correlated from fetal tobacco exposure is attention deficit disorder.

Abuse and Neglect

When we look at the population of students with LD as a whole, more than twice as many have been abused when compared to normal student populations. Failure of parents or guardians to take care of children's physical, educational, medical, or emotional needs is on the rise.

Environmental Toxins

Pesticides, formaldehyde, asbestos, and other toxins contribute to improper brain development. But the most prevalent toxic exposure in children may be lead. Lead exposure in boys is the single greatest predictor for delinquency and the most common indicator for aggression.

Figure 9.1 shows different artistic renderings from two five-year-olds, one of whom was exposed to pesticides. One possible explanation of this discrepancy in exposure is that rainwater washes the residue from high to low and ends up in the valley water supply and crops. Then through consumption of food and water, the toxins are absorbed into the brains of children and wrecks havoc on their internal systems.

Head Injuries

Athletes are more prone to concussions and injuries than nonparticipating individuals. Female soccer players suffer 40 percent more concussions than males. The physicality of the game can lead students into aggressive play, with possible damaging effects to their brain (Covassin, Stearne, & Elbin, 2008).

Touch Deprivation

Insufficient infant stimulation through caressing, holding, touching, and massage can result in impaired motivation to learn, emotional adjustment problems, and delayed cognitive development.

Poorly Treated Ear Infections

While ear infections are relatively common among infants, the frequency, severity, and treatment of them are significant factors in later social and cognitive functioning.

| **Figure 9.1** | The Effects on Preschool Children Exposed to Pesticides |

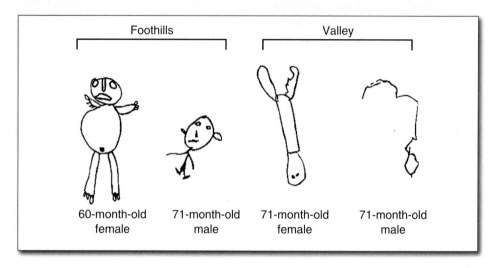

Note the difference between the drawings of five-year-olds: the healthy kid (on left) and the one exposed to greater pesticides levels in the valley (on right).

Source: Guillette, Meza, Aquilar, Soto, & Garcia, 1998.

Undiagnosed Deafness or Hearing Impairment

Some suggest that kids with LD are actually better at auditory processing, yet studies suggest a higher incidence of auditory processing disorders (Charlop-Christy, Carpenter, Le, LeBlanc, & Kellet, 2002).

Maternal Personality Disorders

Mothers with narcissistic, paranoid, or histrionic tendencies or border-line personality disorder are the least sensitive caregivers. In turn, many of these mothers' babies show signs of delayed cognitive development at 6 months of age.

Infant Attentional Problems

Infant visual attention can be measured in relation to performance on memory tasks encompassing visual function. Infants who exhibit pro-longed patterns of fixation appear to be at risk for later cognitive deficits.

Family Interaction Patterns

Variables such as parenting differences (e.g., amount of attention, interaction, type of interaction) are associated with differences in a child's vocabulary and IQ between 7 and 36 months old.

Crowded Living Environments

Studies suggest that parents living in crowded homes speak in less complex, sophisticated ways with their children and are less responsive to them compared to parents in uncrowded homes. Children living in crowded homes are also more likely to be abused.

Brain Areas Involved

Delayed development is not isolated to a specific area of the brain. Rather, it seems to impact the aggregate, including the following systems:

- *Cognitive:* visual-spatial, analytical, mathematical, and creative functioning
- *Emotional:* endocrine system, social, cultural, and aesthetic appreciation
- *Perceptual-motor:* listening, vestibular system, sensory acuity, timing, and state management
- *Stress response:* immune response, autonomic nervous system, sympathetic and parasympathetic nervous systems
- *Memory:* listening, attention, concentration

Recognizable Symptoms

When a child exhibits consistent behavior or developmental patterns that are different from the norm, pay closer attention and note the nature of the behaviors, preferably in writing. What seems to trigger them? Are they consistent? Are you aware of any extenuating circumstances? Once you've made an effort to observe the behaviors, rather than judge them, consider how they might relate to the following characteristics, behaviors, and symptoms.

Cognitive

- inconsistent performance
- often misses the big picture
- slowed problem solving
- weak at cause and effect; might understand even memorize rules but has no idea how or when they apply
- impaired perception
- difficulty in generalizing information
- poor short-term memory
- diminished perceptual skills
- common visual-spatial deficits severe enough to affect academic performance in subjects such as written mathematics
- weaker cognition
- general difficulty with reading comprehension by age 10
- difficulty in specific mathematic areas such as computation and abstract applications
- impaired concept formation
- slowed abstract reasoning

Language and Communication

- pragmatic deficiencies in language usage
- very concrete and very literal
- poor nonverbal communication
- unable to intuit or read between the lines (impacting both conversation and reading comprehension)
- poor social skills; troublemaking; difficulty keeping friends
- may resist participation in group activities
- poor ability to understand the behavior of others

Physical

- physical awkwardness and uncoordination
- often better in individual rather than team sports
- difficulty learning to catch and kick a ball, dance, hop, and skip
- physical difficulties often more pronounced on the left side of the body
- possibly impaired fine motor skills
- handwriting may be poor and/or laborious
- spatial perception problems

Life Skills

- decreased preschool exploratory activity
- hypoactivity
- overdependency on parents
- difficulty adjusting to new situations
- dislikes changes to the routine
- often lacks common sense, or "street smarts"
- can be incredibly naive
- prone to anxiety and depression
- low self-esteem
- often withdrawn, sometimes agoraphobic
- higher than normal incidence of suicide

Fetal Alcohol Syndrome Effects

Size: Growth retardation is below the 10th percentile when corrected for gestational age. These individuals rarely catch up in size, even in an enriched environment.

Central nervous system: Developmental delays and mild retardation are common; the average IQ for a child with FAS is 65 to 85.

Body and facial abnormalities: While often subtle, there are some abnormalities that are highly correlated with FAS, such as a smaller head, a thinner upper lip, clubfeet, cleft palate, and fingerprint abnormalities. Other abnormalities include small size, low birth weight, retarded growth, smaller eye openings, flat midface, short upturned nose, flat elongated grooves above lip, small chin, and simply formed and low-set ears.

Typical symptoms and behavioral patterns include the following:

- difficulty structuring work time
- impaired rates of learning
- poor memory
- trouble generalizing behaviors and information
- impulsivity
- reduced attention span; highly distractible
- fearlessness; unresponsive to verbal cautions
- poor social judgment
- developmental delays in skills such as handling simple money transactions
- trouble internalizing modeled behaviors
- differences in sensory awareness (hypo- or hyperawareness)
- language production that is higher than comprehension
- poor problem-solving strategies
- arithmetic deficits
- academic functioning averages on the second- to fourth-grade levels
- maladaptive behaviors such as poor judgment, distractibility, and difficulty perceiving social cues

Crack-Exposed Babies

The degree of disability varies widely in crack-exposed babies depending on the amount of the original exposure, the timing of it, the comorbidity factors, and the postnatal environment. Environmental factors in early childhood seem to intensify or reduce the severity of the symptoms. Crack-exposed children often move from one foster home to the next, have one or no parents, and have inadequate daycare. Typically, mothers are poor, white, and single. General symptoms and behaviors in crack-exposed babies include the following:

- difficulty processing novel stimuli
- erratic sleep cycles
- easily overaroused and distracted
- less persistent in task completion
- more aggressive and impulsive
- easily distressed
- possibility of speech/language delays

Studies indicate that the single most predictive factor in the severity of symptoms in crack-exposed babies is the quality of home environment after birth. Unfortunately, most addicted mothers are malnourished, exposed to abuse, living in poor housing, lacking prosocial values, and weak in parental affection. As a result, it's not likely that they will sustain a quality, nurturing home environment without intensive intervention/treatment.

Malnutrition

Protein deficiencies can lead to behavior problems. For example, some children perceive hostility where none exists and therefore display inappropriate aggression. Anemia (iron deficiency) is linked to short attention span, disruptive behaviors, and impaired memory. Lack of B vitamins can lead to impaired thinking and memory.

Anesthesia Exposure

There are some indications that the use of obstetrical anesthesia during delivery may result in subtle alterations in the formation of neurons, synapses, and neural transmitters that are undetectable at birth. In one study, exposed infants/toddlers showed increased probability of delays in typical benchmark developmental tasks such as sitting, standing, and walking. And by age 7, they were more likely to lag in language, judgment, and memory skills.

Environmental Toxins

While there are many potential environmental toxins, lead is the most researched one. Lead exposure has been correlated with aggressiveness, irritability, and short-term memory loss.

WHAT YOU CAN DO

Learn what you can about the particular child in question and the suspected disorder. Talk to parents, school psychologists, counselors, physicians, and other mental health professionals. Due to the extent and timing of critical neural development, much of the damage is not reversible. While the human brain is highly plastic and malleable, there are limitations. No pharmacological treatment exists presently for children with FAS. Those with exposure to milder levels of childhood abuse, blows to the head, and/or other trauma have a much higher treatment success rate than FAS victims. The degree of severity, however, varies a great deal. Don't give up on anyone. Environment plays a crucial role in the future gains of the developmentally challenged child. There's a lot you can do!

In these children, the brain's academic operating system is clearly not up to the task of the school's demanding academic environment. It will have to be strengthened. (Strategies for doing so are discussed in Chapter 2 and the next section of this chapter.) Do not get sidetracked in pursuing your plan. Here are the essentials:

1. Believe that it will work; know that the brain can and will change with appropriate interventions.

2. Build a team, and make a plan so that every person is on the same page.

3. Focus on building all aspects of the operating system.

4. Always maintain relationships throughout the process.

5. Be positive and patient. This will take time.

Remember, focus on the student's academic operating system. This means that each part of the operating system becomes a daily focus for you. Everything else you do is secondary. The strategies described in the following section can help turn what might at first feel like a tough or even hopeless situation into a good chance for change. These students will only improve to the degree that their operating system is built up to peer level. More specifically, build hope, processing, sequencing skills, attention, memory, and a champion's mindset. In addition, be sure to use the tips in Table 9.1.

Provide a safe, structured environment with relevant learning activities and high support levels. Do not "dumb down" your class. Rather, incorporate strategies that represent good teaching regardless of special needs. Students with LD just need more high-quality teaching methods on a more consistent basis.

Stay Positive

Success for these students takes time. Because of the enormous plasticity of the early human brain, be positive and hopeful. Many children who are "delayed" catch up (to a degree) later. The primary reason most make only minimal progress is that the intervention was not comprehensive (i.e., broad based, systemic, and lasting). When building an intervention program, be sure to improve students' ability to communicate effectively in everyday contexts. Retrain their visual, speech, motor, and spatial systems. Provide plenty of physical activities and nutrition. Be sure the brain-training program is practiced 30 to 90 minutes a day, three to six days a week.

Allow Students to Make Mistakes

A secret of intervention is to allow students to make mistakes. There is emotion in mistakes. Reinforce the effort and praise with the correction.

Table 9.1	Teacher Tips for Managing Students With LD

- Provide a high level of structure and consistency; routines help learners predict coming events.

- Offer a variety of learning activities that utilize multiple learning styles and intelligences.

- Keep instructions brief and simple; assign less complex projects to students with LD.

- Break large projects down into small steps so that learners don't become overwhelmed.

- Provide advance notice when an activity shift is going to occur; give learners time to prepare themselves mentally and physically for the change.

- Provide plenty of external support structures, such as prompts, written reminders, affirmations, cooperative learning groups, partner sharing, and lists/outlines.

- Be concrete when teaching a new concept; show and tell, and give learners hands-on practice.

- Be positive. With persistence, you will see some improvement, both cognitively and behaviorally.

- Use rituals; create plenty of predictable events daily in class to make learning fun and exciting.

- Get learners' attention through a variety of means, such as music, special guests, and surprises.

- Repeat important information numerous times.

- Articulate learning goals and objectives repeatedly.

- Arrange interventions with specialized training programs and/or tutoring.

- Develop a support team of colleagues and professionals to assist you when necessary.

- Affirm progress and reevaluate goals on a regular basis.

- Model good stress management practices; take personal time out if necessary, pause and do some deep breathing, and when upsets or setbacks occur take a different tack.

- Strive to build open lines of communication with all learners, but especially those with LD.

- Remember, you make a difference.

Making mistakes is crucial when it comes to rewriting the brain. Here's why: neurons commonly interact with thousands of other neurons, and this network refines learning through multiple trials and error recognition. This way you enable an upgrade of students' operating system with error correction, repetition, and reinforcement.

Incorporate the Arts

The arts are excellent builders of the operating system. Musical arts can help train listening, memory, and motor skills. Visual arts help train spatial, sequencing, and creative skills. Dramatic arts instill processing, attentional skills, and volition.

Be Patient and Reduce Stress

Be patient in the process, and keep stress low. A feeling of lack of control drives stress, so provide predictions of upcoming events, coping skills for any changes, assurances of safety, tools for self-control, and likely scenarios of any changes. Take note of and appreciate the small miracles that occur on a daily and weekly basis. When upsets and setbacks occur, take in a deep breath and pause. Affirm progress and set new goals. Concentrate on that which you have control over.

REVISITING THE STUDENT

"Ashley," one of the learners introduced in the pretest at the front of the book, is also the student who fits the profile for LD. Like the others, Ashley is unique—she exhibits a pattern of symptoms that are associated with a specific disorder. However, some of these symptoms can be observed in other conditions as well. This is why you want to look for patterns rather than isolated behaviors. To help you remember what's important in assessing students with LD, take a moment, relax, and focus on the photo, the symptoms, and the key points of this chapter.

Symptoms

- Difficulty structuring work time
- Impaired rates of learning and poor memory
- Has trouble generalizing behaviors and information
- Sometimes exhibits impulsive behavior
- Easily distracted and frequently exhibits reduced attention span
- Displays a sense of fearlessness; is unresponsive to verbal cautions
- Displays poor social judgment
- Has trouble internalizing modeled behaviors
- Language production is higher than comprehension
- Overall poor problem-solving strategies
- May have unusual facial features

SUPPLEMENTAL RESOURCES

Books

All Kinds of Minds, by Melvin Levine

Brain Foods for Kids, by Nicola Graimes

The Edge Effect: Achieve Total Health and Longevity With the Balanced Brain Advantage, by Eric Braverman

Ghosts From the Nursery, by Robin Karr-Morse and Meredith Wiley

Managing Attention and Learning Disorders, by Ian McEwan

Sensory Integration and Learning Disorders, by Jean Ayers

Shadow Children, by Careth Ellington

The Source for Nonverbal Learning Disorders, by Sue Thompson

Students in Poverty: Toward Awareness, Action, and Wider Knowledge, by the Canadian School Boards Association

Web sites

BabyZone: www.babyzone.com

BrainWare Safari: www.brainwareforyou.com (K–12)

LifeSkills Training: www.lifeskillstraining.com (K–9)

Minnesota Learning Resource Center: www.themlrc.org

National Organization on Fetal Alcohol Syndrome: www.nofas.org

Positive Action: www.positiveaction.net (K–12)

Project ALERT: www.projectalert.com (5–8)

Providing Alternative Thinking Strategies (PATHS): www.prevention.psu.edu/projects/PATHS.html (K–6)

SmartBrain Technologies: www.smartbraingames.com (K–8)

10

The Confused Learner

Dyscalculia

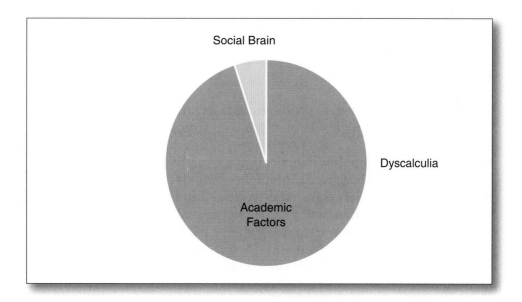

These days, it's the exception to find someone who's good at math. It's more common to find someone who does poorly in math and seems to have a poor "math sense." This means that they don't really compare and contrast numbers well in their head. They rarely can estimate money well, or they lack a general sense of how much and how many.

Dyscalculia is a neurologically based learning disability that affects the processing of numbers (von Aster & Shalev, 2007). The prefix *dys* comes from Greek and means "badly." *Calculia* comes from the Latin *calculare*, which means "to count." More specifically, this term refers to the ability to represent and manipulate numerical magnitude nonverbally on an internal number line. In many ways, this is a spatially oriented capacity to represent the gist of math numbers well. The number line competency typically develops during elementary school. But additional cognitive components are needed to become proficient in math, including working memory, sequencing, processing, and number symbolization (language). There are two subtypes of dyscalculia: difficulties with approximate numerosities and difficulties with exact numerosities.

In contrast, students with good number sense glide seamlessly between the concrete and the abstract. They blend the real world of quantities and the abstract world of numbers and numerical expressions. They can invent their own procedures for conducting numerical operations. They can represent the same number in multiple ways depending on the context and purpose of this representation. They can recognize benchmark numbers and number patterns, especially ones that derive from the deep structure of the number system. They have a good sense of numerical magnitude and can recognize gross numerical errors (i.e., errors that are off by an order of magnitude). Finally, they can think or talk in a sensible way about the general properties of a numerical problem or expression without doing any precise computation.

IMPACT

The greatest impact of dyscalculia, frankly, is on school test scores. Once students are beyond high school, those who struggle with approximation skills are, for example, less savvy in shopping and workplace tasks that require approximation. But in general, it's more of an inconvenience than a serious problem. Those weak in number sense typically find careers that don't require estimation skills. The world is full of calculators and other people who are more than willing to fill the mental gaps. One can get away with a math disability far more easily than a reading or social disability.

Dyscalculia does not come and go, but the severity may range over time. Severity, however, can be environmentally dependent—related, for example, to variables such as teaching style or stress levels. The good news is that the majority of those with dyscalculia learn to effectively compensate for their disability and go on to lead productive and successful lives.

Demographics

Unfortunately, dyscalculia often goes undiagnosed. Approximately 5 percent of children (although estimates vary between 3 and 11 percent) have some degree of dyscalculia, with equal numbers of boys and girls being affected (Shalev & Gross-Tsur, 2001). They have been taught in the same way as their peers and engaged in the same mathematical activities, yet they encounter distinct difficulties in mastering the basics of mathematical thinking. Many teachers would suggest that the number is much higher than what studies show. This may be due to comorbid conditions, such as dyslexia, attention deficit hyperactivity disorder (ADHD), and auditory processing deficits. Although dyscalculia and attention deficit disorder (ADD) are separate conditions, approximately 40 percent of those with dyscalculia also have ADD.

Commentary

Those with dyscalculia don't necessarily hate math, but it is more difficult and time consuming for them. They may avoid it and are often baffled by it. It is encouraging that early detection and intervention increase school success rates in those with dyscalculia. It's important to know the exact nature of the problems you're dealing with. The easiest to notice are students having difficulty dealing with a mathematical-spatial sense, exhibited by the following possible signs:

- difficulty with number and order sequences
- failure to understand the importance of working left to right
- difficulty telling the time on an analog clock
- scattering tally marks instead of organizing them systematically
- confused by division (e.g., Is it 3 into 6, or 6 into 3?)
- in 10s and units, takes the smaller number from the larger, regardless of position
- difficulty rounding numbers
- easily overloaded by pages/worksheets full of figures
- makes copies of work/shapes inaccurately

Conceptually, we have two different notions for numerical abilities. Some research suggests that infants possess a number module, or basic numerosity, that enables them to construct early mathematical concepts (Butterworth, 1999). It's an appealing concept: "Your baby is naturally smart in math!" Yet others have shown that infants are equipped only with a sense of approximate numerosities (Feigenson, Dehaene, & Spelke, 2004), which is especially significant because it is approximations upon which the more robust and school-ready concepts of exact numerosities are constructed. These more specific math understandings are intertwined with the application of language skills, providing the early scaffold and later math-language blend that makes for excellent math skills (Lemer, Dehaene, Spelke, & Cohen, 2003).

These competing proposals have actually been tested, effectively asking: Is it early innate math skills or the combination of math, spatial awareness, and language skills that builds later solid math skills? Researchers assessed whether performance on approximate numerosity tasks was related to performance on exact numerosity tasks. In one study of eight- and nine-year-olds, no relationship was found between exact tasks and either approximate or analog tasks in normally achieving children, children with low numeracy, or children with developmental dyscalculia (Iuculano, Tang, Hall, & Butterworth, 2008). Low numeracy was related not to a poor grasp of exact numerosities, but to a poor understanding of symbolic numerals. This suggests that schools do play a part in the development of these skills and that it's not all up to whether you have a "baby Einstein." (By the way, Einstein was a poor math student until his middle school years. He showed little promise until his uncle helped him with geometry.)

Rarely does only one condition result in failed learning. Many of those with dyscalculia experience comorbid conditions such as depression, learned helplessness, and ADD, which can complicate diagnosis and treatment. You can definitely help these learners, but it would be a good idea to rally additional support.

Likely Causes

The primary cause of developmental dyscalculia (DD) currently appears to be a genetically determined disorder of number sense. Some children with DD that runs in the family show deficits that are limited to number sense only. Yet some children have DD and comorbidities such as language delay, dyslexia, or ADHD (Tressoldi, Rosati, & Lucangeli, 2007). Epidemiological data indicates that two-thirds of children with DD have comorbid conditions, while one-third have pure DD. Good assessment can help you tell the difference. Overall, about 50 percent of the siblings of a pupil with dyscalculia can be expected to have it as well. Parents and siblings of a pupil with dyscalculia are 10 times more likely to have dyscalculia than members of the general population (Shalev & Gross-Tsur, 2001). These findings add convergent support to the evidence mainly obtained from group comparisons that the more distinctive characteristics of dyscalculia are functionally independent of dyslexia.

Brain Areas Involved

A recent brain imaging study showed less brain activity in right parietal gray matter of people with dyscalculia, as well as grey matter abnormalities in regions of the frontal cortex (Ansari, 2008; Molko et al., 2003). These are areas that highly correlate with spatial abstractions, spatial reasoning, problem solving, and mental calculation. There are also higher correlations with low birth weight and susceptibility to dyscalculia, presumably because those areas of the brain may be impaired or underdeveloped, or the family may be less able to provide early childhood enrichment activities that can mitigate any differences (Isaacs, Edmonds, Lucas, & Gadian, 2001). These differences are small but noticeable, which suggests that any changes in the brain that result from favorable, structured practice are clearly surmountable in six months or less.

Recognizable Symptoms

Dyscalculia is a condition that affects the ability to acquire basic math skills, including number sense, which refers to fluidity and flexibility with numbers as well as a comfort level with numbers and the sense of what they mean. Dyscalculia is also affected by the ability to perform mental mathematics and to look at the world and make comparisons. Geary (1999) and Dowker (2003) emphasize the wide variety of difficulties shown in cases of dyscalculia but note that learners affected by it typically show the following:

- difficulty understanding basic number concepts
- lack of an intuitive grasp of numbers
- problems learning number facts and procedures
- tendency to work more mechanically and without confidence
- poor estimation skills

You probably recognize by now that there are diverse and multiple phenomena associated with dyscalculia and that the condition can range from mild to severe. No two students with dyscalculia exhibit exactly the same physiology. Butterworth's (2003) *Dyscalculia Screener* identifies deficiencies (indicated by slow reaction times) in two processes: counting dots and comparing the value of numerals. There is solid correlation between poor performance on those two tests and poor mathematics performance (using the nfer-Nelson mental mathematics tests; Clausen-May, Claydon, & Ruddock, 1999). As stated previously, there may be comorbidity with other problems (e.g., ADHD), but those two indicators are a primary key. Thus, clinicians can look for a narrow range of symptoms.

The differences become obvious over time. One student may start school knowing that 9 is 4 bigger than 5, whereas his or her peers (with less well-developed number sense) may simply know only that 9 is bigger than 5. Some children may have an amazing number sense, even being able to figure out how much bigger 9 is than 5 using fingers, talking it out, or counting blocks. Many with dyscalculia answer the question "How many?" with the last word used in counting, despite not understanding how counting works. However, the children who have mastery of the cardinal principle understand that adding objects to a set means moving forward in the numeral list. They also understand that subtracting objects mean going backwards. Those with dyscalculia don't usually understand that adding exactly 1 object to a set means moving forward exactly (and only) 1 word in the list. In short, if you sense something is "off," there's a good chance it is.

Difficulties With the Words and Symbols of Mathematics

- rarely ask questions, even when they evidently do not understand
- very tough to generalize learning from one situation to another
- make mistakes in interpreting word problems
- difficulty talking about mathematical processes
- get mixed up with terms such as *equal to* and *larger than*

Slower Mental Calculation

- difficulty estimating or giving approximate answers in working
- forget previously mastered procedures very quickly
- recite the entire multiplication table to get an answer for a simple problem
- rely on tangible counting supports, such as fingers and tally marks
- complete multiplication tables by "adding on"
- forget the question before the answer can be worked out
- use the "counts all" method instead of "counting on" for addition
- difficulty remembering basic mathematics facts
- can't remember what different symbols mean

Spatial-Visual Gaps

- lose track when counting/reciting tables
- difficulty navigating back and forth, especially in twos, threes, and so on
- confused about the difference between, for example, 32 and 23
- put numbers in the wrong place when redistributing or exchanging
- poor setting out of calculations and of work on a page
- difficulty remembering the steps in a multistage process
- may not be able to locate a number on a number line without searching up and down
- failure to notice visual patterns such as the 0 in 10, 20, 30, 40
- can't relate to visual representation of fractions/decimals such as circles divided in half

Reliance on Imitation and Rote vs. Understanding

- can "do" sums mechanically but can't explain the process
- sometimes use the wrong working method, such as treating a 10 as a 1 (or vice versa) in exchanging or redistribution
- can't decide what arithmetical operation is required
- can't build on known facts (e.g., may work out that 3 + 4 = 7 but not realize that, therefore, 4 + 3 = 7 as well)

- frequent difficulty with arithmetic, confusing the signs +, −, ÷, and ×
- difficulty with everyday tasks (e.g., checking change, reading analog clocks)
- inability to comprehend financial planning or budgeting, sometimes even at a basic level (e.g., estimating the cost of items in a shopping basket, balancing a checkbook)
- difficulty conceptualizing time and judging the passing of time

WHAT YOU CAN DO

Dyscalculia is not a disease; time, nutrition, enrichment, or medication will not curb or cure it. Rather, dyscalculia is the result of a different style of thinking and learning, and is best addressed through retraining the brain with skill building, behavior modification, and tutoring. Spend extra time on math as a whole. Start early and be persistent. This can be treated successfully.

In cases of dyscalculia, the brain's academic operating system is clearly not up to the task of the school's demanding academic environment. It will have to be strengthened. (Strategies for doing so are discussed in Chapter 2 and the next section of this chapter.) Do not get sidetracked in pursuing your plan. Here are the essentials:

1. Believe that it will work; know that the brain can and will change with appropriate interventions.

2. Build a team, and make a plan so that every person is on the same page.

3. Focus on building all aspects of the operating system.

4. Always maintain relationships throughout the process.

5. Be positive and patient. This will take time.

Teach Numeracy

Teach numeracy at all levels, not just from kindergarten to second grade. Despite mandates in many districts to provide numeracy training for educators, most teachers simply don't emphasize numeracy skills. There are more than one hundred basic math facts to be memorized to automaticity in order to support early scaffolding in building a brain with numerosity skills.

Use quality assessments to find out whether students "froze up" on the latest math test.

Provide One-on-One Support

Students with dyscalculia are highly likely to require focused, one-to-one teaching to support what is taught in the classroom.

Help Students Stay Organized

Having a neat and uncluttered workspace is imperative to helping students with dyscalculia learn.

Show Patience

Do not overstress the importance of mathematics in daily life or in academic advancement. Do the opposite: make learning relaxed and fun.

Choose Words Carefully

Children's mathematical concepts are intertwined with their language development. Teach students the functional (not abstract) meaning of words such as *more, less, bigger, longer, twice, before, after, the same as,* and *enough* by using various objects as well as their bodies.

Use Plenty of Naming and Self-Talk

Teach students to count and name shapes out loud. (Parents can support this process well before students start school.) Language is key to thinking ahead (e.g., "I'll have to work out how many bananas there are, and then I can divide that number by the number of people to find out how many each one can have.").

Turn Early Math Concepts Into Tasks, Objects, or Demonstrations

Children with dyscalculia may not understand silly rhymes or acronyms (e.g., "Six takes two, you can't do, so borrow a ten") when they can't grasp the concepts behind them. Use fingers, Legos, dice, beads, cards, small candies, and other concrete objects to help students learn concepts such as more, less, same, bigger, and smaller. Ask them to talk through their thinking in order to embed the reasoning. Give real-life math examples to support their understanding and memory. Concrete always will beat abstract. Other interventions may include adapting pictures into the math curriculum to illustrate and help children comprehend better and be able to remember later. Let students get into a "number line" in class, showing the order of numbers from top down based on ages or a drawn or assigned number.

Teach Reasoning Skills

Children with dyscalculia can use logic and have good verbal skills, but poor spatial skills. Learning number facts as derived facts, related to patterns and relationships with other number facts, is more likely to be effective than learning by rote.

Simplify the Times Tables

Teach the times tables in the form of a pyramid, with ten equations across the bottom (1×1, 1×2, 1×3, etc.). The next row across has just nine across, because one of equations was already learned below ($1 \times 2 = 2 \times 1$). Each row across has fewer and fewer equations until the top row has just one, $10 \times 1 = 10$. The advantage of this process is that students will memorize just 50 percent of the total that they used to learn and they learn the reverse of each, too (e.g., $4 \times 7 = 7 \times 4$). This builds numerosity and saves time.

Use Talk-Alouds and Meta Thinking

Learning math facts that are connected through discussion and subsequent reasoning is a good strategy for checking students' work. Talking aloud allows you to ask questions and helps students better generalize what they learn. Explain why a process, step, or strategy works, and help students apply them correctly in different situations.

REVISITING THE STUDENT

"Courtney," one of the learners introduced in the pretest at the front of the book, is the student who fits the profile for dyscalculia. Like the others, Courtney is unique—she exhibits a pattern of symptoms that are associated with this specific disorder. However, some of these symptoms can be observed in other conditions as well. This is why you want to look for patterns rather than isolated behaviors. To help you remember what's important in assessing students with dyscalculia, take a moment, relax, and focus on the photo, the symptoms, and the key points of this chapter.

Symptoms

- Has difficulty with number and order sequences
- Understands the importance of working left to right
- Finds telling the time on an analog clock difficult
- Scatters tally marks instead of organizing them systematically
- Gets confused with division (e.g., is it 3 into 6, or 6 into 3?)
- Gets easily overloaded by pages/worksheets full of figures
- Makes copies of work/shapes inaccurately

SUPPLEMENTAL RESOURCES

Books

Dyscalculia: Action Plans for Successful Learning, by Glynis Hannell

Dyscalculia Guidance, by Brian Butterworth and Dorian Yeo

Dyscalculia Screener: Highlighting Children With Specific Learning Difficulties in Maths, by Brian Butterworth

The Dyscalculia Toolkit: Supporting Learning Difficulties in Math, by Ronit Bird

Early Numeracy: Assessment for Teaching and Intervention, by Robert J. Wright, Jim Martland, and Ann K. Stafford

Elementary Mathematics and Language Difficulties, by Eva Grauberg

Individual Differences in Arithmetical Abilities: Implications for Psychology, Neuroscience, and Education, by Ann Dowker

The Number Sense: How the Mind Creates Mathematics, by Stanislas Dehaene

Web sites

About Dyscalculia: www.aboutdyscalculia.org

Audiblox: www.audiblox2000.com/

GL Assessment, Dyscalculia Screener:
shop.gl-assessment.co.uk/home.php?cat=314

EdTech Software, Bubble Reef:
www.edtech.ie/details.asp?id=15690&ptid=20041

Learning in Motion, To Market, To Market:
www.learninginmotion.com/products/market/index.html

The Mathematical Brain: www.mathematicalbrain.com

National Center for Learning Disabilities: www.ncld.org

Softpedia, The Number Race:
mac.softpedia.com/get/Educational/The-Number-Race.shtml

White Space, NumberShark: www.wordshark.co.uk/numbershark.html

11

The Unsound Learner

Central Auditory Processing Disorder

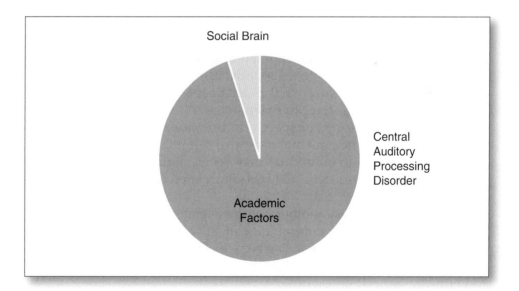

M any of the brain differences create confusion and chances for a false diagnosis. For example, we've all seen kids who turn to their neighbors and start talking or asking questions when they are supposed to be on task, but what if those distracting behaviors were actually symptoms of a serious academic issue? A key part of the brain's academic operating system is the capacity to pay attention and process information. That's exactly what many students struggle with, and the result is a real problem.

Central auditory processing disorder (CAPD) is a deficiency in the information processing of audible signals not attributable to impaired peripheral hearing sensitivity or intellectual impairment. The individual with such deficits experiences limitations in the ongoing transmission, analysis, organization, elaboration, storage, retrieval, and use of information contained in auditory signals (Rosen, 2005).

The terms *central auditory processing* and *auditory processing* are interchangeable, as are *auditory perception, central deafness, word deafness, auditory comprehension deficit,* and *auditory perceptual processing dysfunction.* The factors that influence auditory processing are auditory attention, auditory memory, motivation, maturation and integrity of the auditory pathways, decision processes, and use of linguistic cues such as grammar, meaning in context, and lexical representations. As a result, learners with CAPD generally are less able to pay attention and follow directions. In addition, they are often hyperactive, easily distracted, and easily frustrated. Kids with CAPD may have normal hearing, but parts of the brain that analyze and interpret sensory information from the ears do not function appropriately.

IMPACT

Speech and language problems are often the earliest indicators of a learning disability. People with developmental speech and language disorders have difficulty producing speech sounds, using spoken language to communicate, or understanding what other people say. The most common auditory subdeficit is receptive language disorder—the inability to understand certain aspects of speech. In this case, the individual's hearing is fine, but he or she can't make sense of certain sounds, words, or sentences. As a result, the individual may seem inattentive. As you might also guess, reading disorders are highly correlated with auditory processing deficits.

Articulation disorder, another auditory-related problem, is characterized by the inability to control rate of speech and articulate words. Learners with this disorder may lag behind classmates in learning to make speech sounds (e.g., at age 6 a child may say "wabbit" instead of "rabbit" and "thwim" instead of "swim").

Developmental articulation disorders are common, too. Fortunately, these are often outgrown or successfully treated with speech therapy. Expressive language disorder—a language impairment that is characterized by difficulty expressing oneself in speech—is also common. In this case, the student often calls objects by the wrong names, speaks only in two-word phrases, and/or can't answer simple questions clearly.

Demographics

The number of learners impacted by auditory-processing deficits (including speech and language disorders) varies depending on age group. The percentage of students with this disorder fluctuates also in relation to economic and environmental background, family size, toxic exposure, and geography. By adulthood, the number of individuals still suffering from auditory-processing deficits decreases to 5 to 7 percent of the general population.

Commentary

Listening and hearing are not the same. Hearing is a physiological process involving the detection of sound, whereas listening involves an active attentional process and requires complex skills sets. Listening, comprehending information, and expressing oneself adequately are integral skills for success in school and life.

Kids with CAPD struggle because auditory processing is the foundation of all other forms of educational processing, such as understanding language, processing information, and learning content. For learners who have an auditory-processing deficit, trying to function in school can be so chaotic and difficult that it is not uncommon for them to develop additional chronic problems as a result. This is why early intervention is so important. Once the problem is identified, coordination between caregivers and educators is critical. An appropriate remedial plan needs to be agreed upon by all parties and put in place as quickly as possible. Auditory-processing deficits represent a moderate level of challenge to the classroom teacher. You can contribute to the success of learners with CAPD, but you will need support from others, notably a speech pathologist and a learning specialist.

Likely Causes

Heredity

There is speculation that faulty prenatal neuronal migration in the first trimester may lead to underdevelopment of auditory-processing capabilities. Family history appears to be a potential factor as well. It is not uncommon for children with auditory-processing deficits to have a sibling or other family member with similar difficulties.

Frequent Ear Infections

Frequent and severe inner ear infections can also have an adverse effect on the development of auditory-processing capabilities. Age of onset, number of episodes, duration, and treatment effectiveness are all factors that influence the long-term impact and severity of childhood ear infections.

Left-Hand Dominance

Family handedness is another consideration that is being explored. Some research suggests that a left-hand preference can be a diagnostic indicator of CAPD.

Hypersensitivity to Loud Sounds

Children with auditory-processing deficits often exhibit a lower tolerance for loud sounds due to abnormal central suppression effects. Likewise, learners with attention deficit disorder (ADD) also exhibit significant differences in their preference for comfortable listening levels and tolerance of loud sounds. This raises the question of whether children with attentional disorders may have central suppression deficits that need to be evaluated for appropriate management in the classroom.

Atypical Hearing Loss

CAPD is a disruption of neural integration functions. This commonly includes out-of-sync arrival times of the electrical impulses from the two cochlea through the brainstem to the brain. Since speech is dependent on time, any delays of time from one ear over the other can cause a child to hear distorted sounds.

Brain Areas Involved

Frontal and Parietal Lobes

Although auditory processing is typically assigned to the temporal lobes, the frontal and parietal lobes also play a role (see Figure 11.1). The frontal lobes are involved in executive decision making, which includes planning, focus, anticipation, and task distribution. These functions are necessary for auditory processing because the brain makes hundreds of decisions every minute about how much attention to give to each of the incoming sounds that a person hears. In addition, the lower areas of the parietal lobes process meaning from the sounds we hear. This combination of frontal-parietal function helps students sort out and make meaning of the many sounds in a busy classroom.

Inner Ear

Problems associated with cochlear hair cells and/or the auditory nerve may be indicative of an auditory-processing deficit as well. Some studies suggest that a lack of activity in the auditory nerve causes nerve endings to assume a different shape, typified by more branching and smaller terminal swellings. The new shape is one typically associated with hearing problems. Impulse traffic is a critical factor in the interaction between the ear and central auditory stations and appears necessary for the maintenance of key synapses. Once again, we have environmental stimuli impacting a probable genetic defect.

Figure 11.1   Organization of the Human Brain for Language

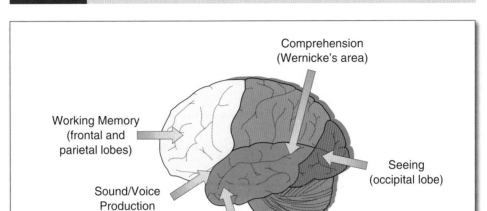

Comprehension
(Wernicke's area)

Working Memory
(frontal and
parietal lobes)

Seeing
(occipital lobe)

Sound/Voice
Production
(Broca's area)

Word Memory
(temporal lobes)

Recognizable Symptoms

Children with auditory processing deficits generally experience difficulties in speech, language, and/or learning, especially in the areas of spelling and reading. (Consult Table 11.1 for a checklist of symptoms indicating CAPD.) The impact on speech may be subtle. Some children who have difficulty hearing the difference between speech sounds or confuse syllable sequences will manifest this difficulty in their pronunciation.

In addition to these verbal problems, students with auditory-processing deficits face many kinesthetic challenges, including difficulties with listen-and-perform activities (e.g., the Hokey Pokey). This problem can carry over to other learning tasks that have a series of ordered steps. For example, a student may have difficulty putting a musical instrument back into its carrying case and putting it away.

Auditory verbal-memory tests can underestimate true memory performance, particularly in individuals with unknown hearing status. Most information communicated in the classroom (at all levels) is auditory, and much casual learning is auditory as well. By the time a child is ready for fourth grade, most auditory discrimination, speech and language development, and memory and processing skills are mature and intact, except in children with CAPD.

School hearing screening usually uses fixed intensity of about 20 dB at as few as four frequencies. Failure criteria are set at one low frequency missed (which indicates possible middle ear loss) and two high frequencies (which indicates possible nerve damage). Auditory-processing disorders can occur in a single high frequency. This can still cause hearing loss.

Table 11.1	Symptoms Indicating Auditory-Processing Concerns

These symptoms may indicate an auditory-processing deficit:

- delayed speech (no words spoken by the child's first birthday)
- mixed-up speech (in multisyllabic words)
- trouble rhyming (by age four)
- chronic difficulty with directionality (e.g., left versus right, over versus under, before versus after)
- behaves as if peripheral hearing loss is present (even though hearing sensitivity is normal)

These symptoms may indicate a hearing impairment:

- inattentive
- easily distracted
- frequent head turning (for better hearing)
- retrieval problems ("Um . . . I forget the word.")
- difficulty following oral directions
- omission of word endings
- speaks with words out of order
- mistaken words (e.g., "Starvation Army" instead of "Salvation Army," "fum" instead of "thumb")
- poor academic functioning
- may have significant history of middle ear pathology

General symptoms of auditory processing concerns:

- may refuse to participate in classroom discussions or may respond inappropriately
- may be withdrawn or sullen
- exhibits poor reading and/or spelling skills
- has other fine and/or gross motor skill deficits
- has verbal IQ scores lower than performance scores
- exhibits poor musical skills
- has difficulty with basic communication skills, sequencing, social judgment, gestalt patterning, and spatial abilities
- has difficulty perceiving subtle auditory cues that underlie the communication of humor, intonation, sarcasm, and intent

WHAT YOU CAN DO

Refer students with suspected CAPD to a speech-language pathologist for testing. They need to be at least 7 years old to get an evaluation for CAPD. They must demonstrate significant scatter across the subtests assessed by speech/language and/or psychology educational tests, with weaknesses in auditory-dependent areas. Find the right person to test these students. Speech pathologists can help collaborate with audiologists in overall screening and assessment; however, audiologists are the professionals who are qualified to determine the presence of CAPD.

Without the processing skills intact, students will consistently struggle with some of the most basic skills such as listening, decision making, and problem solving. Make sure you get help because this issue is treatable. Remember, this dysfunction of the brain impairs a key part of the academic operating system, which clearly is not up to the task of the school's demanding academic environment. It will have to be strengthened. (Strategies for doing so are discussed in Chapter 2 and the next section of this chapter.) Do not get sidetracked in pursuing your plan. Here are the essentials:

1. Believe that it will work; know that the brain can and will change with appropriate interventions.

2. Build a team, and make a plan so that every person is on the same page.

3. Focus on building all aspects of the operating system.

4. Always maintain relationships throughout the process.

5. Be positive and patient. This will take time.

But beware: misdiagnosis for CAPD is common. The comorbidity of CAPD and ADD and dyslexia is very high. There is strong evidence that auditory processing plays a major role in the etiology of dyslexia, but it does not cause it. The initial diagnosis that children receive sometimes depends on whether they are seen by an audiologist or a psychologist.

Two approaches to treatment are commonly used. One focuses on improving the hearing, or how well the ear talks to the brain. The other concentrates more on rebuilding functional everyday processing (e.g., directions, vocabulary words, conversations). This latter approach is geared toward how well the brain understands what the ear tells it. Each of these approaches has its advocates—one focusing on input, the other on output.

There are a few auditory skill-building approaches that can be implemented. The Berard approach uses selected high and low frequencies from a music source and then sends sounds via headphones to the student. The Tomatic approach uses an Electronic Ear to regulate latency time, precession, and auditory laterality. It retrains the ear to enable a person to hear oneself and uses the voice to sensitize and retune the hearing. This is also called Samonas Sound Therapy.

If students have a middle-ear condition, they will not be able to represent and rapidly access individual sounds in words. This condition is known to affect central auditory performance and, therefore, needs to be assessed before more sophisticated tests can be done. These students will most likely require special training. Other intervention programs, including Earobics, Fast ForWord, NeuroNet, Balametrics, and Interactive Metronome, are good to research and implement.

Many learners can hear just fine in most ranges, but certain sounds go by too fast. Sounds from words and phrases like *tabulate* and *back too late* may sound the same to them. Software programs can stretch out the sounds in words so that learners can better hear them. With practice, many of these students will eventually be able to meet the high-speed processing demands of conversation.

A speech and language therapist can also help in the areas of speech production, discrimination of speech sounds, language comprehension, and direction following. Hearing speech with the presence of miscellaneous noises is testable.

The following classroom suggestions can ease the stress and aid the learning of individuals with an auditory processing disorder:

- Reduce noise.
- Provide a quiet environment to help learners with auditory-processing deficits hear better.
- Improve acoustics in the room with acoustic noise buffers, draperies, or carpets.
- Move learners with CAPD away from auditory and visual distractions to help them focus and maintain attention.

Maintain Close-In Seating

Seat these students close to the teacher and blackboard, and away from windows, doors, and other potential noise distractions.

Use Visual Prompts

Be sure to continually augment verbal instructions and information with visual displays. You can also help learners with processing disorders by looking directly at them while speaking. This allows them to read your body language and lips, if necessary.

Provide Hearing Training

Involvement with a speech-language pathologist usually improves these learners' classroom functioning. The pathologist can provide additional support in the areas of phonology, grammar, vocabulary, and world knowledge, which helps learners fill in the blanks that frequently evade the "unsound learner."

Focus on Meaning

Focus more on meaning versus separate words in the initial presentation of material. For example, when reading to children, emphasize the feelings and drama in the story. This helps learners better encode the information and improves recall. On subsequent readings of the material, the words themselves can be emphasized.

Communicate Clearly

Get feedback on your teaching often by using choral response, repetition, and pair sharing. Break instructions down into simple, concise, concrete actions. Give students time to process and organize the information with pauses in your speech and slowing down the amount of information you deliver.

Convey messages with clear verbals (key words, overviews, and reviews) and clear nonverbals (cues, signs, and prompts). Select fewer key words to emphasize. Avoid asking learners to listen and write simultaneously. Provide clear instructions and then review them. Vary the volume and tonality of your voice as well as your facial expressions. Check in with learners frequently to determine whether your message was heard the way it was intended and to reinforce it. For example, you might quiz them with a question such as "How many minutes did I say we have for this task?"

REVISITING THE STUDENT

"Brent," one of the learners introduced in the pretest at the front of the book, is the student who fits the profile for auditory processing disorder. Like the others, Brent is unique—he exhibits a pattern of symptoms that are associated with a specific disorder. However, some of these symptoms can be observed in other conditions as well. This is why you want to look for patterns rather than isolated behaviors. To help you remember what's important in assessing students with auditory-processing deficits, take a moment, relax, and focus on the photo, the symptoms, and the key points of this chapter.

Symptoms

- Inattentive to others
- Easily distracted
- Engages in a lot of head turning to hear better
- Retrieval problems ("Um. . . I forget the word.")
- Difficulty following oral directions
- Omits word endings
- Speaks words out of order
- Mistaken words—says "starvation army" instead of Salvation Army or "fum" instead of thumb

SUPPLEMENTAL RESOURCES

Books/Journals

When the Brain Can't Hear, by Teri James Bellis

The Workings of the Brain: Development, Memory, and Perception, by Rodolfo Llinas

Central Auditory Processing Disorders, by Deborah Kelly

Sensory Integration and Learning Disorders, by Jean Ayers

Journal of Learning Disabilities

Web sites

Audiblox: www.audiblox2000.com

BrainSkills: www.brainskills.com

Bungalow Software: www.bungalowsoftware.com

Lindamood-Bell Learning Process: www.conceptimagery.com

Staff Development for Educators: www.sde.com

Sound Listening Corporation: www.soundlistening.com

Wright Group: www.wrightgroup.com

12

The Impulsive Learner

Attention Deficit Hyperactivity Disorder

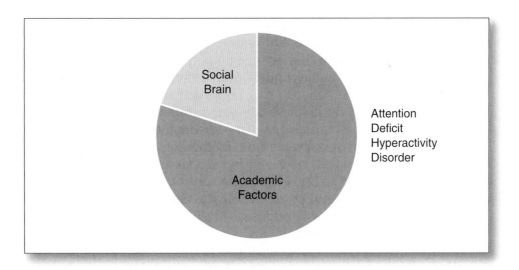

M ost young kids have difficulty focusing and staying still. Kids are up and around so often we call them antsy. But when a child is significantly less able to focus than his or her peers, it may be a case of attention deficit hyperactivity disorder (ADHD). This is the condition characterized by memory issues, impulsiveness, and time disorientation.

Attention deficit can occur with and without hyperactivity. Without hyperactivity, kids tend to be impulsive cognitively, but physically they remain stationary and unfocused. As of late, the number of cases of attention deficit with hyperactivity has overshadowed the former. Here we'll focus on the most common occurrence of attention deficit, ADHD. The National Institute of Neurological Disorders and Stroke defines ADHD as a neurobehavioral disorder that interferes with a person's ability to stay on task and to exercise age-appropriate inhibition (cognitive alone or both cognitive and behavioral).

In 2003, ADHD became the number-one diagnosed school-age disorder in the United States. Prevalence estimates in school-age children have ranged from 2 to 18 percent in community samples (Pastor & Reuben, 2005). However, there is some difficulty in explaining the variances in diagnosis of ADHD. For example, symptoms might be interpreted differently by different cultures, symptoms may not be disabling in the context in which they are measured, there may be secondary gains or losses in labeling students, symptoms may be masked by other acute disorders, and students' home life may make it difficult to assess.

ADHD occurs more frequently and with greater consequences than is typically observed in others at a comparable level of development. It is not a disease; do not blame the person or trivialize the condition. Students with moderate to severe cases are highly at risk for behavioral, emotional, and academic failure, but those with ADHD can and do succeed with proper diagnosis, intervention, and support.

Given the time frame of kids diagnosed with ADHD, it is important to know that all ADHD behaviors can be considered normal for some people, at some age, for a certain time. But with ADHD, these behaviors are the rule, not the exception, and they are age inappropriate.

To fully understand and accurately diagnose ADHD, it is necessary to consider the age of the sufferer. It is important to identify the various criteria—severity, early onset, lifestyle onset, duration, impact, and setting. (See Table 12.1 for the clinical qualifiers for diagnosing a student with ADHD.) In four- and five-year-olds, both inattention and hyperactivity are likely dominant symptoms; however, by age six or seven, the primary problem typically shifts to one of impulse control. Students with ADHD may know what to do, but they are not always able to do it because of an inability to manage their own responses. This does not, however, mean they are not smart or not learning.

The U.S. government has legislation in place for individuals with ADHD. The Individuals with Disabilities Education Act (IDEA) states that a student with ADHD must undergo a two-pronged test, may or may not need direct services, and the disability must interfere with the student's learning processes. Additionally, according to IDEA Section 504 (the Civil Rights Division, Disability Rights Section), if ADHD severely affects the child's learning, then a service plan is needed.

It should be noted that ADHD is a psychiatric diagnosis, not a disability category as recognized by IDEA (Salend & Rohena, 2003). At present, no laboratory test exists to determine whether a child has this condition.

Table 12.1	Criteria for Diagnosing ADHD: Clinical Qualifiers

- onset before the age of 7
- diagnosis often delayed until problems manifest in school
- problems exhibited in two of three settings (e.g., home, school, office)
- can rule out other potentially similar psychiatric disorders (e.g., oppositional defiant disorder, sensory integration disorder, central auditory processing disorder, learning delays, schizophrenia, stress disorders, psychosis, trauma)

Source: American Psychiatric Association, 2000.

You cannot diagnose ADHD with urinalysis, a blood test, EEG, PET, fMRI, or SPECT scan, though these can help. It is important to look at the student's complete health history before making any diagnosis. Rule out look-alike or confusing conditions, such as seizure disorder, Tourette syndrome, specific learning disability, vision acuity problem, child psychiatric problems, middle ear infections (causing hearing problems), central nervous system abnormality, and stress disorders.

Untreated ADHD carries its share of risks, including academic underachievement, legal problems, substance abuse, social difficulties, and risky behaviors. Consider a few of these statistics in regards to students with ADHD:

- 35 percent will drop out.
- 5–10 percent will complete college.
- 40–50 percent will engage in antisocial activities.
- 50–70 percent have few or no friends.
- 70–80 percent will underperform at work.
- They are more likely to experience teen pregnancy and sexually transmitted diseases.
- They are at greater risk for excessive speeding and car accidents.
- They have a higher risk for depression and personality disorders (Barkley, 2002).

IMPACT

The ADHD diagnosis carries with it significant implications for families, educators, and, of course, those who are diagnosed with it. Only a licensed professional, such as a pediatrician, psychologist, neurologist, psychiatrist, or clinical social worker, can make the diagnosis that a person has ADHD.

Over the past 40 years, educators and medical specialists have seen an increase in the number of learning disability diagnoses among school-age children. In the case of children with ADHD, the most effective treatments include an accurate diagnosis, a compatible/flexible environment, and a combination of medication and behavioral therapy, if necessary. Left untreated or misdiagnosed, ADHD can have a long-term adverse impact on children and their academic, social, and emotional well-being. It is best to diagnose ADHD while observing children over a period of time.

Demographics

At the elementary school level, boys are more than twice as likely as girls to have been diagnosed with ADHD (9 percent versus 4 percent, respectively). By age 14, girls are identified with the condition more than boys. Many critics have suggested that elementary school seems better designed for girls than boys (Biederman, Faraone, & Monuteaux, 2002).

Growing up with ADHD does not mean a lifetime of medication. Eighty to 90 percent of sufferers do not need medication as adults (Barkley, 2002). The majority of children with ADHD grow up and do well. As little as 10 to 20 percent have significant impairment and disability.

Income disparity might also attribute to the child diagnosed with ADHD. In 2003, 15 percent of children in families receiving welfare had been diagnosed with ADHD, compared with 6 percent of children in families not receiving welfare. ADHD should ideally be diagnosed in a child who lives in a stable social environment, not one raised in a highly chaotic social environment, because high instability often produces symptoms that mimic ADHD, thus making diagnosis difficult (Morrison, 1995). This suggests that poverty and stress may make even a healthy, typical child present ADHD-like symptoms.

Studies also suggest that ethnicity plays a part in ADHD. Proportionally, more whites are diagnosed with ADHD than nonwhites. In 2003, 8 percent of non-Hispanic white children and 6 percent of non-Hispanic black children had been diagnosed with ADHD, compared with only 4 percent of Hispanic children. These disparities suggest the possibility that income and cultural differences may affect both perceptions and analysis of behaviors associated with the condition (Pastor & Reuben, 2005).

Commentary

Comorbidity is common in ADHD sufferers. They often qualify for other diagnoses. Almost 33 percent of children with ADHD also have more than one comorbid condition. More often than not, ADHD presents itself with other cognitive and behavioral issues, including the following:

- oppositional defiant disorder
- conduct disorder
- dyslexia

- anxiety and mood disorders
- depression
- learning disorders
- Tourette syndrome
- obsessive-compulsive disorder (National Institute of Mental Health, 1996)

The prevalence rates of comorbid ADHD are high. Estimates of various comorbid conditions in children with ADHD range from 12 percent (learning disorders) to 35 percent (oppositional disorders) to as much as 92 percent (conduct disorders; Osman, 2000). Current literature indicates that approximately 40 to 60 percent of children with ADHD have at least one coexisting disability (Jensen et al., 2001).

Likely Causes

Understanding ADHD requires examining a multitude of factors, including genetic, environmental, and nongenetic issues. (See Figure 12.1 for an in-depth illustration of the brain's functional differences in students with ADHD.) Possible etiology-related explanations for ADHD include child-rearing tactics, nutrition changes, stress and anxiety, and prolonged screen and computer time.

Genetic

ADHD is genetically transmitted in 70 to 95 percent of all cases. It tends to cluster in families, with a greater incidence with first- and second-born relatives. Twin and adoption studies show strong genetic correlations, but the relationship is not predictable or causal. There is also molecular evidence in several studies that link candidate genes to ADHD (Ding et al., 2002).

Physiology

Scientists have found that specific areas in the frontal lobe and basal ganglia of ADHD patients show a reduction in both size and activity of about 10 percent. These areas of the brain were understimulated when scientists took brain images of people with ADHD. However, students do not have to undergo a brain scan in order to receive an ADHD diagnosis.

Chemical Dysregulation

Some ADHD research has implicated the neurotransmitter dopamine. Dopamine pathways in the brain, which link the basal ganglia and prefrontal cortex, appear to play a major role in ADHD. Insufficient "fuel" or stimulation in the prefrontal cortex prevents this part of the brain from playing its standard impulse-regulation role. However, since antidepressants are

| Figure 12.1 | A Working Model for ADHD |

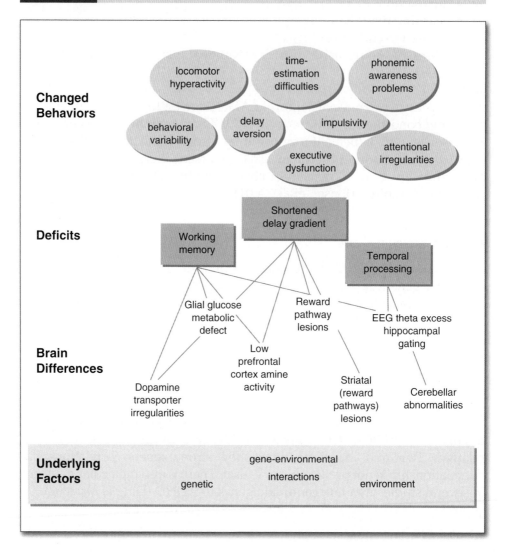

Source: Adapted from Kieling, Goncalves, Tannock, & Castellanos, 2008.

often successful in treating ADHD, this raises questions about misdiagnosis and/or serotonin involvement.

Head Injury

Although the skull is hard, the brain is soft. And upon impact, the brain can be launched into its hard casing, making it very susceptible to damage. The typical growing-up experience presents countless possibilities for injury: a fall from a bike, bunk bed, tree, or roof; a car accident; a sports injury; a fight; or physical abuse. Every one of these incidents can put a child at risk for developing learning and conduct problems later on.

Why? The area that regulates impulse control, the prefrontal cortex, is the area of the brain most easily damaged.

Frontal-Lobe Symmetry

Some ADHD research has implicated oversymmetry between the left and right frontal lobes. In general, the left frontal lobe is more involved with approach behaviors and the right frontal lobe with avoidance behaviors. In normal subjects, the right frontal lobe is a bit larger than the left, which would seem to indicate a stronger tendency toward avoiding negative repercussions (or stronger impulse control).

Other Potential Risk Factors

A multitude of nongenetic factors might play a part in ADHD. Environmental toxins or allergens, pre- and postnatal cerebral pathology (e.g., fetal exposure to alcohol, drugs, or tobacco), birth complications, and head injury (Kollins, McClernon, & Fuemmeler, 2005; Slomine et al., 2005) are such factors worth examining in these students.

Childrearing Changes

Close, nurturing parenting is needed from birth to age five as the brain has higher vulnerability to environmental influences (Rice & Barone, 2000). In 1960, an estimated 10 percent of all children were in childcare. Today, over 60 percent of all kids will spend time in childcare (Molko et al., 2003), which increases the potential that they may not receive sufficient parental nurturing. Additionally, the added pressures of distractions such as fast-paced television shows and violent images amp the developing brain's response. Less chaotic images and a less stressful upbringing may help the brain develop differently (Christakis & Wright, 2004).

Nutrition

The quality of food intake attributes to brain function, with some studies linking, for example, excess sugar and poor diet with behavioral problems in children (Benton, 2007; Jacobson, 1996). Among infants under 24 months old, one in nine has french fries daily and one in four has hot dogs daily (Fox, Pac, Devaney, & Jankowski, 2004). Children who eat more processed foods with preservatives, additives, and trans fats risk adverse health effects, both short-term and long-term, such as Type 2 diabetes and an early onset of obesity. Good eating habits (e.g., consuming fresh fruits and vegetables, legumes, and whole grains) and portion control lead to a life-long commitment to healthy living. Also, high-protein foods (e.g., eggs, lean meats, yogurt, soy, nuts, whole grains) provide tyrosine, which is converted into uppers like dopamine and noradrenaline to boost the brain's neural activity in the frontal lobes.

Some students with ADHD take medication, such as methylphenidate (Ritalin), which increases dopamine, or Straterra, which increases norepinephrine. The good news is that diet alone may support these processes. Additionally, specific dietary supplements may include amino acid tyrosine, essentially fatty acids, and phospholipids. Tyrosine is used for conversion into dopamine in the brain (Harding, Judah, & Gant, 2003).

Brain Areas Involved

Overall, children with ADHD have brains that are different from typical brains. (See Figure 12.2 for an illustration of the brain's structures involved when someone has ADHD.) There is evidence of neurotransmitter imbalances (Castellanos & Acosta, 2004), lower cerebral blood flow (Lou et al., 2004), and anatomical differences (Castellanos & Acosta, 2004). MRI scans have found a range of abnormalities in brain development associated with ADHD. Brains are 3 to 4 percent smaller in the frontal lobes, temporal gray matter, posterior inferior vermis, caudate nucleus, and cerebellum (Castellanos & Acosta, 2004).

Neural Pathways

Converging evidence from multidisciplinary studies of ADHD suggests involvement of frontostriatal circuitry, which is involved in the ability to inhibit impulsivity (Durston, 2003). Altering the brain's wave states

| **Figure 12.2** | Brain Structures Involved With ADHD |

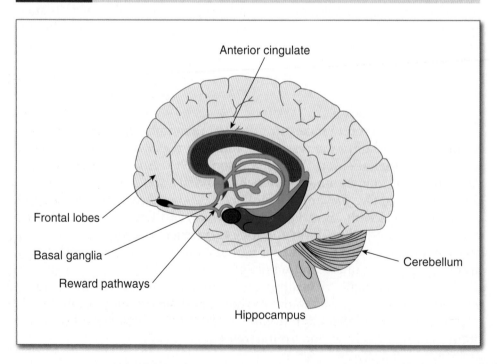

increases the activity and speed of processing (see Figure 12.3). Amphetamines work for many with ADHD because those with the disorder spend far more time in the theta brain wave area. When "speed" is added to the brain, the frontal lobes increase brain wave activity to alpha or beta.

Prefrontal Cortex

The most common symptoms of ADHD are all associated with the frontal lobes and/or prefrontal cortex. These symptoms include lack of impulse control, critical learning from experience, perseverance, disorganization, poor self-monitoring, and weak social skills.

Blood Flow and Brain Activity

PET scan studies suggest abnormalities in catecholamine function in ADHD. Underactivity of the aminergic system in such regions may lead to deficits in attention and activity level.

| Figure 12.3 | Understanding Specific Brain Wave States |

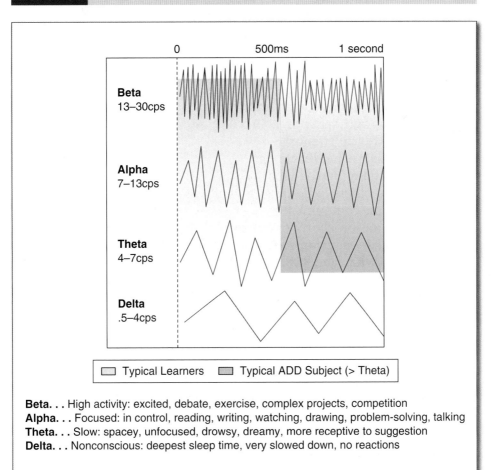

Beta. . . High activity: excited, debate, exercise, complex projects, competition
Alpha. . . Focused: in control, reading, writing, watching, drawing, problem-solving, talking
Theta. . . Slow: spacey, unfocused, drowsy, dreamy, more receptive to suggestion
Delta. . . Nonconscious: deepest sleep time, very slowed down, no reactions

Biochemistry

Biochemistry is usually an issue with ADHD patients. The rate at which the brain uses glucose—its main energy source—is lower in subjects with ADHD. There is also an imbalance, usually with amines (uppers). For example, they show a depressed release of dopamine (Volkow et al., 2002), and less dopamine means poor working memory vis-à-vis frontal lobe function. That's the last thing kids with ADHD need since their frontal lobes are underpowered as it is. Amphetamines (e.g., caffeine, norepinephrine, Ritalin, Adderall) are all uppers for the brain, as is dopamine. In the right dosage, these can enhance focus, attention, and working memory.

Recognizable Symptoms

Kids with ADHD exhibit a persistent disabling pattern of behavior as well as memory impairment; impulsivity; and poor prediction, planning, and reflection skills. In school-age children with ADHD, you may see the following:

- rushing into tasks but not finishing them
- demanding attention from adults
- inability to delay gratification
- moodiness
- often getting into trouble with adults
- feeling disorganized, lost, and "dumb"
- aggression and defiance
- poor short-term memory
- weak at following directions
- asking another person what was just said
- looking at others to figure out what was said
- late for time commitments
- desk is a mess—poorly organized
- forgetting about promises made
- knowing what and how but not when and where to do it—it's appropriateness
- spacey, poor concentration
- weak time orientation
- inability to plan ahead
- poor at reflecting on past
- makes the same mistakes over and over
- poor time management
- inability to curb immediate reactions
- act before thinking
- hit or grab first, then realize it later
- blurt out inappropriate comments

- nearly impossible to wait for things—little or no patience
- always wants to be in motion
- can't sit still, dash around
- squirm, wiggle, and touch everything
- not focused—try to do several things at once

A complete assessment is usually best conducted by a developmental pediatrician, a pediatric neurologist, or a psychiatrist in conjunction with a qualified psychologist.

WHAT YOU CAN DO

ADHD should be taken seriously. These sufferers are at high risk for academic and social failure, consequences that can be avoided with proper intervention. Since ADHD frequently coexists with other problems, diagnosis is sometimes tricky. Vision and/or hearing problems need to be ruled out first. Students with ADHD frequently have a specific learning disability as well. They may have trouble mastering language, reading, math, or performing handwriting. Focus on the ADHD student's strengths and provide extra support wherever needed.

Remember, in cases of ADHD, the brain's academic operating system makes it tough to succeed in the school's demanding academic environment. It will have to be strengthened. (Strategies for doing so are discussed in Chapter 2 and the next section of this chapter.) Do not get sidetracked in pursuing your plan. Here are the essentials:

1. Believe that it will work; know that the brain can and will change with appropriate interventions.

2. Build a team, and make a plan so that every person is on the same page.

3. Focus on building the operating system. In this case, focus on memory, attention, and delayed gratification.

4. Always maintain relationships throughout the process.

5. Be positive and patient. This will take time.

The strategies described here can help turn what might at first feel like a tough or even hopeless situation into a good chance for change. Trying to fix or cure ADHD is counterproductive. These students are not broken; rather, they need understanding and accommodation. Although ADHD is not always considered a learning disability, its interference with concentration and attention make it very difficult to perform well in school. More serious perhaps is the fact that many boys with ADHD also have oppositional defiant disorder; these students can be very stubborn and belligerent, and have frequent angry outbursts that make them difficult to manage in class.

ADHD can also progress to the more serious conduct disorder. Students with this combination of problems may fall into serious legal trouble. They may steal, set fires, destroy property, or act out violently; they may act recklessly and take undue risks. Students who exhibit these antisocial behaviors should be promptly referred to the school psychologist or other medical/mental health professional.

Many experienced educators, by virtue of necessity, have learned to accommodate learners with ADHD. What do they do? First and foremost, they maintain a positive attitude. They also tweak the balance between control/direction and student empowerment. And when they are in over their head, they make the appropriate referral. The accommodations you learn to make for learners with ADHD also benefit the rest of your students. Managing this condition effectively requires good basic teaching skills.

Use Different Levels of Treatment

When treating ADHD, what is the goal? The goal is to change the student's behavior, of course. All ADHD behavior change focuses on strengthening the frontal lobes, which can be done chemically or behaviorally. When ADHD is mild to moderate, the following interventions may be highly effective without the use of medications:

- nutritional support
- lifestyle coaching
- skill building
- neurofeedback
- environmental changes
- student asset-building

Mainstream treatments for those with ADHD, when it is moderate to severe, are multimodal in scope and likely include medication. The multimodal treatment approach consists of the following:

- patient, parent, and teacher education
- medication (the class of drugs called stimulants)
- behavioral therapy
- environmental supports, including appropriate classroom accommodations

Provide Accommodations

It is essential to understand the conditions and accommodate students with ADHD. If you are a new teacher, the challenge will be greater, as you'll have more on your plate and your stress level may be higher. But remember, the best way to effectively manage students with ADHD is to provide a positive learning environment that focuses on their strengths rather than their weaknesses. Be flexible, but maintain consistent boundaries on important issues, such as those that involve their own and others' safety.

Here are some specific strategies for dealing with short-term memory issues:

- Repeat instructions if necessary.
- Break tasks into small units.
- Set realistic deadlines for each task.
- Make lists of what you need to do.
- Preplan the best order for doing each task.
- Make a schedule for doing tasks.
- Establish your routines and stick to them.
- Create high predictability through daily and weekly events that always happen on cue.
- Start the same way, transition the same way, and end the same way.
- Add variation only when it's acknowledged as a change.

And here are some accommodations for ADHD students with organizational challenges:

- Use a calendar/planner to keep on track.
- Write down things you need to remember.
- Write different kinds of information in different sections.
- Keep the book with you all the time.
- Post notes to yourself—tape notes on mirrors, refrigerator, locker, and so on.
- Store similar things together.
- Create a routine.
- Use small travel clocks.

Refer Out as Necessary

If you suspect that students with ADHD may have a comorbid condition, promptly refer them to the school psychologist and/or another medical/mental health professional. This is your call, and it's an important one. Ask yourself, "Can I handle this student? Am I skilled enough? Is the student otherwise healthy and happy?" If the answers are yes, the following strategies may be enough to manage the student without intervention. If, however, the answer to any of these questions is no, then seek appropriate help.

Use a Behavior-Modification Approach

Focus on reinforcing positive behaviors and rechanneling negative ones. Behavior modification is most effective when done immediately when the behavior occurs. If you attend to it later, students aren't likely to internalize the information. Obviously, you can't always be at the side of students with ADHD, but you can create an infrastructure that supports them as much as possible (e.g., star charts, extra privileges, self-checklists, cooperative teams, partner grading, numerous feedback mechanisms). Pinpoint one or two behaviors to focus on at a time so that the students (and you) don't get too overwhelmed and tired. Choose your battles carefully.

Avoid Threats/Distress

Too much pressure causes the ADHD sufferer's brain to shut down and underperform. This is why a gentle and moderate approach is best. Rather than making threats like "If you don't stop talking, you're going to have to stay after school," say "Let's set three goals that we want to accomplish today. In five minutes, I'll check back with you to see if you're on track." You never want to embarrass students for their ADHD behavior. It is not by choice; they have a disorder. These students are different, but then again, aren't we all in one way or another?

Provide External Reinforcers

Since students with ADHD have a much harder time with delaying gratification than average students, provide plenty of external motivators. Good motivation tools include a points system, a star chart, peer approval, extra recognition, responsibilities, and/or privileges. Acknowledge progress, appropriate behaviors, and goal achievement. Encourage parents to use similar motivators.

Establish Routines

Create high predictability through daily and weekly events that always happen on cue. For example, provide a daily overview of the lesson plan, open class the same way each time, transition from one activity to the next in a routine way, end class with a predictable closure, and make one or more days out of the week special in some way (e.g., Monday "Goal Setting" Session, Wednesday "Check-In" Session, Friday "Celebration"). When the routine varies, acknowledge the change ahead of time.

Incorporate More Movement

Include plenty of movement and hands-on activities in your lesson planning. Vary the types of movements from sitting to standing to walking to running. To control inappropriate behavior, limit free time. Establish a signal system that students with ADHD understand so that communication with them can be either verbal or nonverbal. A signal should be agreed upon to indicate to them that it's time for them to take a walk once around the building. Make sure that they know you expect them back within five minutes.

Sharpen Communication

Important information such as ground rules, grading policies, team/group divisions, and upcoming events, should be posted in writing in obvious locations around the classroom. Make it as easy as possible for learners to access information. Keep oral instructions brief and repeat them, provide written instructions (and review them orally) for multistep processes, and divide learning tasks and homework into steps.

Manage Information Flow

Teach learners how to manage information so that they don't become overwhelmed. Show them how to scan and review reading material, how to focus on first and last sentences and paragraphs, and how to break tasks into chunks. Provide helpful self-check criteria and/or daily checklists, show them how to proof their work before turning it in, and help them set up a planning calendar or notebook (listing homework assignments and due dates, textbooks/supplies needed, etc.). Write out instructions for them, and repeat important information. Teach them memory tricks (mnemonics) like writing key words in the air and associating something they want to remember with a silly or novel visual image.

Increase Feedback

Focus on students' strengths and successes. Acknowledge even partial progress. Don't wait until mastery is achieved to praise them. Use external motivators like progress charts and points systems, in which good behavior earns points toward classroom privileges. Make a practice of catching the student being good. Incorporate group activities to increase peer feedback.

Teach Time–Management Skills

Teach students how to break up learning tasks into chunks and manage them with an external reminder system (e.g., planning calendar, notes, computer programs). Help students manage their time in the classroom with prompts, pointers, timers, bells, and timekeepers. Be sure to clarify your time expectations for assignments so that there are no surprises. Provide ample warning when a transition from one activity to another is about to occur. A buddy system can sometimes reduce impulse-control problems and provide additional support for students.

Functionalize Classroom Space

Consider creating stations in the classroom for various functions (e.g., reading or writing without distraction, listening to soothing music, engaging in hands-on activities). At the very least, provide a cozy "student office" space where working quietly and independently is encouraged. Room dividers, storage cabinets, bookcases, or simple plastic boxes can be easily adapted for this purpose.

Involve the Entire Class

Hold class meetings to address behavior topics that are especially relevant to ADHD, such as respect, breaking bad habits, problem solving, and noise levels. Be careful, however, not to single out students with ADHD. You might introduce a topic or theme each Monday that will be addressed throughout the week. Facilitate a discussion about how it feels to be disrespected, interrupted, or bullied by others. To be maximally effective, introduce only one topic at a time.

Recommend Behavioral Therapy

Just because a student is on Ritalin or Adderall does not mean the ADHD has been effectively treated. Students who get behavioral therapy in conjunction with medication usually best adapt to the classroom culture.

REVISITING THE STUDENT

"Jason," one of the learners introduced in the pretest at the front of the book, is the student who fits the profile for ADHD. Like the others, Jason is unique—he exhibits a pattern of symptoms that are associated with a specific disorder. However, some of these symptoms can be observed in other conditions as well. This is why you want to look for patterns rather than isolated behaviors. To help you remember what's important in assessing students with ADHD, take a moment, relax, and focus on the photo, the symptoms, and the key points of this chapter.

Symptoms

- Rarely finishes his work
- Calls out answers in class; never waits his turn
- Easily and consistently distracted
- Exhibits weak follow-through and preparation for future events
- Wants everything right away; has no patience
- Personal area (desk) is a mess
- Doesn't seem able to reflect on the past in order to learn from it
- Doesn't sit still; always on the go
- Can't hold several thoughts at a time
- Hindsight or foresight rarely evident

SUPPLEMENTAL RESOURCES

Books

The ADD/ADHD Behavior Change Resource Kit, by Grad Flick

The ADD/ADHD Checklist, by Sandra Rief

All About ADHD, by Linda Pfiffner

How to Reach and Teach ADD/ADHD Children, by Sandra Rief

Ritalin-Free Kids, by Judyth and Robert Ullman

Taking Charge of ADHD: The Authoritative Guide, by Russell Barkley

Your Defiant Child: 8 Steps to Better Behavior, by Russell Barkley

Web sites

Centers for Disease Control and Prevention: www.cdc.gov

Children and Adults With Attention Deficit/Hyperactivity Disorder: www.chadd.org

National Attention Deficit Disorder Association: www.add.org

National Institutes of Health: www.nih.gov

13

The Frustrated Learner

Dyslexia

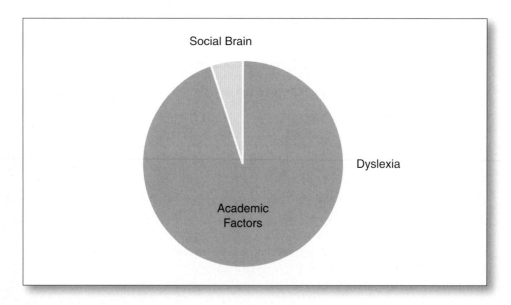

Our society values reading. Without reading skills, one is significantly handicapped, and nowhere more so than in a school environment. While you can describe reading problems in countless ways, the most common is the label of dyslexia. Dyslexia describes a neurologically based learning disability that affects the acquisition and processing of language. It is most notably known as a specific reading disability or a linguistic disorder. Students with dyslexia have normal intelligence, which makes it harder to diagnose as a specific problem. The diagnosis of dyslexia is used to describe a cluster of chronic difficulties in age-appropriate reading skills despite access to instructional, linguistic, and environmental opportunities. It can include broader reading acquisition problems, such as the inability to interpret spatial relationships or integrate visual and auditory information; however, it doesn't encompass all reading problems.

Dyslexia is the most commonly diagnosed reading disorder and does not preclude talent or IQ (Davis, Knopik, Wadsworth, & DeFries, 2000). It involves the inability to develop the capability to read at an expected level, despite an otherwise typical intellect. There is a wide range in the severity of dyslexia—it's more of a spectrum disorder than a clear-cut decision (see Table 13.1 for an outline of subtypes).

Dyslexia can range from a minor disability, such as reflected in a disturbed understanding of what is read, to a complete and pervasive inability to read despite adequate intelligence. Those with moderate to severe dyslexia are highly at risk for behavioral, emotional, and academic failure. Due to the fact that reading is highly valued, untreated dyslexia means both academic risks and the possibility of developing secondary issues, such as low self-esteem. Dyslexia does not go away as children grow up. The studies are clear: it is very likely to persist into adulthood unless successful treatment is received. Many adults with dyslexia simply choose professions in which reading is not a necessary factor. Deficits in phonological coding continue to characterize dyslexic readers later in life (Shaywitz et al., 2007). With intervention earlier in life, however, most students effectively adapt to the impairment.

The terms *reading disability* and *dyslexia* are often used interchangeably, but a subtle distinction between the two does exist. Dyslexia is characterized by impaired development of reading ability, despite an otherwise normal intellect. It is not mentioned directly in the *Diagnostic and Statistical Manual of Mental Disorders* (American Psychiatric Association, 2000) as a disorder except as a 315.00 Reading Disorder, Axis III. The diagnosis of dyslexia is used to describe severe difficulties in reading acquisition despite access to instructional, linguistic, and environmental opportunities. It does not encompass all reading problems. While dyslexia is called a primary reading disorder, there are also secondary disorders as a result of the dyslexia. Secondary disorders may include environmental deprivation, educational deprivation, low self-esteem, depression, and even disease.

Conversely, reading disorders are often characterized by cognitive impairment caused by congenital, environmental, or pathological problems. For example, reading disorders may result from mental retardation, hearing problems, visual problems, environmental and/or educational deprivation, or disease. Because there is no standard test for dyslexia, the diagnosis is usually made by comparing reading ability with intelligence and standard reading expectations.

Table 13.1	Subtypes of Dyslexia

- *Deep dyslexia:* characterized by a constellation of symptoms, including semantic errors (e.g., misreading *angry* for *mad*), an inability to pronounce nonsense words (e.g., *nupeltot*), and an impaired ability to comprehend abstract words in comparison to concrete words (e.g., *cement* vs. *sidewalk*)

- *Surface dyslexia:* characterized by difficulty sounding out words when reading aloud (e.g., words with irregular pronunciations, such as *yacht, island,* and *colonel*)

- *Alexia:* characterized by slower letter-by-letter reading; related to the disconnection of the right hemisphere's visual-information system from the left hemisphere's word-recognition system

- *Neglect dyslexia:* characterized by failure to explicitly identify the initial portion of a letter string (e.g., substitute one word for another if the endings are the same)

- *Attentional dyslexia:* characterized by deficits in short-term memory and the preservation of single-word meanings even in the context of a different sentence meaning; rate deficits in short-term memory may involve spatial and lexical defects in verbal short-term memory

Most people with dyslexia display poor writing ability as well as reading difficulties, and they are often, but not always, poor spellers. However, poor spelling ability alone does not indicate dyslexia. Competent readers are often below-average spellers. Some of those with dyslexia will read notes and numbers correctly but see printed words upside down, backwards, or distorted in some other way. They may have trouble naming letters but not copying them.

Outside of the United States, many educators do not use the term *dyslexia*. They point out that dyslexia is a broad term, which isn't very helpful in developing a targeted educational program to meet a child's individual needs. They might use terms for more specific disabilities, such as *language processing disorders* or *word recognition and decoding disorder,* so they can better choose the most effective instruction and assistance for the child.

Without treatment, students with dyslexia are at greater risk for life's challenges. It is possible to identify dyslexia early and accurately. We can now provide highly effective treatments that lead to skilled reading. Those with dyslexia also may have unique gifts to offer. They are overrepresented in architecture, music, design, theater, and visual arts. Remember that history is full of those who were different—people with dyslexia are different, and their difference can be a gift.

IMPACT

Studies indicate that kindergarten students diagnosed with dyslexia achieved lower grades in school and are less likely to graduate on time.

However, lack of motivation is not the problem; it simply becomes more difficult for these students to keep up. Currently, some funding laws and district policies prohibit school intervention (pullout) programs for students before age nine (or third grade). This can be problematic for the dyslexic reader. Another problem is that to meet the criteria for dyslexia, a gap of about 20 points between IQ and reading achievement must be shown. This definition, however, does not take into consideration that dyslexia can be present in mild forms. Many slightly dyslexic, marginal readers could benefit from early treatment, but unfortunately due to out-dated assessment standards, they don't meet the criteria.

Dyslexia does not come and go. Typically, the condition sticks around, but the severity may range over time. Severity, however, can be environmentally dependent—related, for example, to variables such as teaching style or stress levels. Educators ought to manage reading progress in the same way a doctor manages a patient's high blood pressure—treat the problem immediately while searching for underlying causes. The good news is that the majority of those with dyslexia learn to effectively compensate for their disability and go on to lead productive and successful lives.

Demographics

Unfortunately, dyslexia often goes undiagnosed. The U.S. Department of Health and Human Services estimates that 15 percent of students might have dyslexia. With no specific diagnostic tool to identify the condition, and no universal definition of it, accurate statistics in terms of its prevalence are difficult to come by. The statistics that are published are not consistent, but they paint a picture of the general problem.

A disproportionate number of boys have dyslexia. Although this may actually be a reflection of gender bias. It's possible that teachers more frequently report behavioral difficulties (which are a symptom of dyslexia) among boys in the classroom than from girls. In a large sample size population of students from the Connecticut Longitudinal Study, incidence of dyslexia was identified as 8.7 percent among boys and 6.9 percent among girls. From the same population, teacher-identified incidence was 13.6 percent among boys and only 3.2 percent among girls (Shaywitz et al., 2007). This suggests that boys may be overidentified and/or girls may be underdiagnosed.

Commonly, boys act out their frustrations and girls retreat from attention. Until a universally agreed-upon definition and evaluation instrument is identified, a precise understanding of dyslexia will be difficult.

Although dyslexia and attention deficit disorder (ADD) are separate conditions, approximately 40 percent of those with dyslexia also have ADD. It is unknown at this time what the common neurology is; however, there are clearly some attentional and impulsivity issues related to both conditions.

Commentary

The reasons for dyslexia are varied. They might include exhibiting "gaps" in circuitry and having poor connectivity in the brain. Those with dyslexia don't necessarily dislike reading; on the contrary, many actually love to read. It's just more difficult and time consuming for them. It is encouraging that early detection and intervention increase school success rates in those with dyslexia.

Rarely does only one condition result in failed learning. Many of those with dyslexia experience comorbid conditions such as depression, learned helplessness, and ADD, which can complicate diagnosis and treatment. You can definitely help the dyslexic learner, but it would be a good idea to rally additional support.

Because there is no universal definition of dyslexia and no standardized test for it, it is difficult to arrive at a consensus from the literature regarding the incidence of the disorder. The most common cited numbers are that about 10 to 15 percent of the elementary school-age population has dyslexia (Shaywitz et al., 2007). In a 13-year study of K–12 students in 26 states, 74 percent diagnosed with dyslexia in third grade still had it in ninth grade. Of those students, only 26 percent got successful dyslexia treatment (Shaywitz et al., 2007). The earlier we expect children to be competent readers, the greater the number of disabilities we will discover. Sometimes the brain is just not ready for an academic task on demand.

Income differences might also attribute to incidence of dyslexia. Children from lower-income families have a higher incidence of reading problems than those from middle- to upper-income families (Maulik & Darmstadt, 2009; Riccio et al., 2001). Middle- and upper-income parents are more likely to have books available in the home, which has been shown to be a major predictor of reading success later in life.

Likely Causes

The primary problem to be solved is that of poor connectivity. This is a brain that is not well connected. There are other issues, though, including processing deficits. The prevailing theory in dyslexia is that it is most likely the result of a multisystem brain-based deficit (Habib, 2000). These deficits show up most dramatically as a general impairment in skill automatization. Specifically, the dyslexia deficit shows up in a task that requires the processing of brief stimuli in rapid temporal succession (Fisher & DeFries, 2002). This demand exceeds the capacity of the visual, auditory, and memory areas of the brain designed to handle the task.

Heredity

Reading disorders tend to run in families, so there is likely a genetic component. Several genetic markers have been identified as potential components of the condition, and chromosomes 1, 2, 6, and 15 have been identified as the likely carriers. Multiple studies show strong genetic components: improper migration of cells, ectopic neurons (Galaburda, 1993), prenatal hormone imbalance (James, 2008), and temporal processing deficits (Habib, 2000). Dyslexia, however, is most likely caused by a combination of external and genetic factors.

Auditory-Processing Deficits

Dyslexia is highly correlated with auditory-processing deficits. People with dyslexia exhibit weak attentional capture of new auditory information, prolonged attentional dwell time, and sluggish attentional shifting—all three of which result in poor reading skills. Those with dyslexia also exhibit impaired functioning of the visual system, which feeds the auditory area of the posterior parietal lobes—a combination of problems also believed to contribute to the problem.

Phonological Awareness Problems

Dyslexia is also correlated with weak phonological awareness, characterized by an inability to represent and rapidly access individual sounds in words. It is sometimes evidenced by a deficiency in one or more (but not all) of the following phenomena: sound localization and lateralization, auditory discrimination, auditory pattern recognition, recognition of temporal aspects of audition, auditory performance decrease with competing and/or degraded acoustic signals. This is the area targeted by software programs like Earobics and FastForWord. Individuals with phonological awareness problems may hear just fine in most ranges, but certain sounds go by too fast for them to process. For example, they might not be able to hear the differences between *ba, ta* and *ka* when verbalized at a normal rate. As a result, spelling words properly is difficult.

Inner-Ear Dysfunction

A common thread among those with dyslexia is dysfunction in the cerebellar-vestibular pathway. The inner ear acts as a fine-tuner for all motor signals (balance, coordination, rhythm) leaving the brain and all sensory and related cognitive signals entering it. Because many people with dyslexia also have poor balance, sensory-motor dysfunction, spatial-temporal deficits, and coordination and rhythm deficits, their eyes struggle with the eye-movement motions of reading.

Visual System Dysfunction

While many studies have focused on phonological and inner-ear deficits, there is also support for differences in the regional functional organization of the cortical visual system. Those with dyslexia not only show differences on task performance with visual motion detection, but fMRI scans also show significant activation differences.

Scotopic Sensitivity

A very small percentage of people with dyslexia also have light or sco-topic sensitivity. They have a hard time seeing small black print on white paper; the print appears to shimmer or move. Some are distracted by the glaring white space. These learners tend to dislike florescent lighting and often shade the page with their hand or head when they read. Those with dyslexia see patterns but struggle with motion.

Visual Memory Problems

Another theory suggests that dyslexia represents an inability to rapidly access and retrieve names for visual symbols—a significant transfer failure attributed to phonological difficulties in word sound segmentation. This means, for example, that even when subjects are taught the words *boat* and *far,* they cannot reliably sound out similar-sounding words such as *moat* and *car.* Some studies also indicate abnormal processing of visual motion, which is associated with anomalies in the magnocellular visual subsystem. This system is involved in the detection and processing of low-resolution information. And still other research suggests that dyslexia may be caused by defective nerve cells, which form a pathway from the retina to the brain's visual cortex.

Environmental Possibility

At this time, there are no credible studies that support a hypothesis for an acquired form of dyslexia. However, many life events can predict or exacerbate reading difficulties. These may include, but are not limited to, head trauma, visual or auditory impairments, and damage to memory areas.

Brain Connectivity

Reading takes place all over in the brain. Language-activated cortical regions are found throughout the prefrontal cortex and along the anterior part of the temporal lobe in the left hemisphere. Large variability exists in the exact distribution of activation within a given anatomical area across subjects during reading (Poeppel et al., 2004). See Figure 13.1 to view different brain activations among readers.

Anomalous or sluggish brain connectivity between the brain's two language centers, Wernicke's area and Broca's area, might be an underlying cause of dyslexia. A complex task such as reading requires precise functioning and flow of information between multiple brain sites, including the auditory areas, the visual areas, and the rest of the brain.

In typical children, reading causes activation of the occipital cortex first, then the basal aspect of the temporal lobe, and finally the left posterior temporal and parietal region (Wernicke's area). In children with dyslexia, the third step is replaced by activation of the right side of the

| Figure 13.1 | Different Brain Activations in Typical Readers Versus Dyslexic Readers |

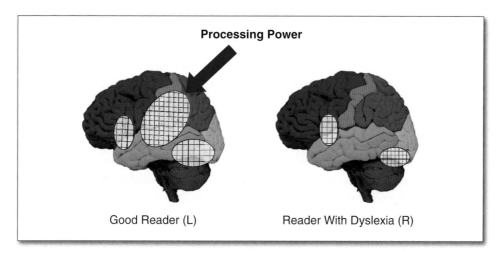

brain instead, the mirror image of the typical route, with very low levels of activity in Wernicke's area (Richards & Berninger, 2008).

Prenatal Deviations

The brains of those with dyslexia may differentiate abnormally while still in the womb. This theory implicates deviations in neuronal pruning and neuronal migration during the second trimester of pregnancy. Some suspect that frontal lobe cells being in the wrong place at the wrong time because of improper cell migration is to blame.

Abnormal Neural Activity

As revealed by PET scans, the dyslexic brain is less energy efficient. Underactivity in the back half of the temporal lobe and a heavier reliance on the frontal lobe (expressive language function) have been noted, impacting both Wernicke's and Broca's areas. Also, studies reveal intensified brain activity in the right hemisphere during reading exercises, while the left hemisphere, which is normally used for reading, remains dormant. Those with dyslexia have been shown to use 4.6 times more brain area to do the same language task as normal controls. Struggling dyslexic readers have a difficult time rhyming—a key skill in reading—and have an overactive Broca's area, where speech is produced.

Brain Areas Involved

Temporal and Parietal Regions

Functional imaging studies of people with dyslexia have indicated reduced regional cerebral flow in the temporal and inferior parietal regions of the brain. Parietal asymmetry is also commonly found in those with dyslexia.

Wernicke's area is where phonological processing and rapid whole-word comprehension occurs. Those with dyslexia show activation in Wernicke's area in terms of verbal short-term memory, rhyming tasks, and phonological processing, but not in concert with other areas (Paulesu et al., 1996). As a generalization, those with dyslexia have less connected brains overall, but they are still malleable.

Corpus Callosum

The left-right transfer of information helps a person understand metaphors and analogies, and match up visual and auditory information. Some studies reveal an enlarged corpus callosum in people with dyslexia, one that is thicker and more rounded than normal. Others show oversymmetry between left and right hemispheres.

Right Occipital Cortex

Studies of those with dyslexia also suggest a specific low-level visual processing deficit in the right occipital region.

Left Occipital Lobe

A congenital brain lesion in the left occipital lobe has been shown to cause developmental surface dyslexia, which, as previously described, is characterized by having difficulty sounding out words when reading aloud.

Inner Ear/Cerebellar-Vestibular System

Inner-ear dysfunction has been found to characterize a large sample of people with dyslexia. The cerebellar-vestibular system is highly involved in sensory input and output as well as balance and coordination. Dysfunction in this area may scramble signals, and even normal brains will have difficulty processing poorly scrambled or distorted signals. The resulting symptoms are dependent on the degree of signal scrambling, the location and function of the varied normal brain centers receiving and processing these scrambled signals, and the brain's compensatory ability for descrambling.

Recognizable Symptoms

You probably recognize by now that there are diverse and multiple phenomena associated with dyslexia and that the condition can range from mild to severe. No two people with dyslexia exhibit exactly the same physiology. Presently, the Auditory-Analysis Test is the most sensitive evaluation instrument available to identify the condition. This test asks subjects to segment words into underlying phonological units and then delete the specific requested phonemes. Such phonological skills are the best current predictor of reading ability. Generally, if a student shows two or more warning signs and there is a family history of dyslexia or ADD, a thorough assessment should be provided when the child is in first grade.

The many ways in which a person can be impaired in the processing of language suggests that there are probably a number of different ways that the brain can be organized (or disorganized as the case may be). Thus, clinicians look for a "constellation" or cluster of symptoms in the following areas:

Memory

- poor memory; quick learner but quick forgetter
- weak in rote memorization and rapid oral retrieval
- extreme difficulty memorizing nonmeaningful facts
- difficulty following oral directions and remembering instructions
- general memory instability for spelling, grammar, math, names, dates, and lists or sequences such as the alphabet, days of the week, months of the year, and directions
- memorization is often very difficult

Visual Processing

- reversals of letters such as *b* and *d*, words such as *saw* and *was*, and numbers such as 6 and 9 or 16 and 61
- letter and word blurring, doubling, scrambling, movement, omission, insertion, size change, and so on
- tendency to skip over or scramble letters, words, and sentences
- poor concentration, high distractibility, light sensitivity, tunnel vision, and/or delayed visual (and phonetic) processing
- difficulty recognizing letters, words, or numbers

Phonological Processing

- slow to catch subtle differences in sounds of words
- mixes up sounds in multisyllabic words (e.g., *am-in-nall* for *animal*, *mawn lower* for *lawn mower*, *buh-sketti* for *spaghetti*, *flustrated* for *frustrated*)
- inability to rhyme by age four
- inability to correctly complete phonemic awareness tasks

Writing

- messy, poorly angulated, or drifting handwriting prone to size, spacing, and letter-sequencing errors
- motor-coordination deficits associated with a disposition to make dysphonemic spelling errors (impaired timing precision identifies a behavioral phenotype in some familial dyslexia subtypes)
- difficulty writing the alphabet in order
- spelling errors will match reading errors

Reading

- slow and fatiguing reading
- compensatory head tilting, near-far focusing, and finger pointing
- sequencing difficulties
- difficulty with multiple-choice questions and long-timed reading passages, as it takes more time to process the words

Cognition

- spoken or written language taken literally; problems with generalization— applying information to new or different situations
- difficulty learning the names and/or sounds of letters and writing the alphabet in order
- inability to work with or be playful with word sounds, rhymes, and sound-alikes

Speech

- slurring, stuttering, minor articulation errors, poor word recall
- auditory input/motor output speech lags
- delayed speech (no words spoken by the child's first birthday)
- impaired timing precision in motor action (impinges on reading and writing deficits in developmental dyslexia)

Kinesthetic Processing

- difficulty learning tasks that have a series of ordered steps, such as tying shoes
- chronic difficulty with many aspects of directionality, such as confusion with left and right, over and under, before and after
- poor follow-through; problems prioritizing and completing tasks; wasting time
- lack of dominant handedness (switching hands between tasks or even while doing the same task)
- impaired timing precision in bimanual coordination and in motor speech

WHAT YOU CAN DO

Remember, when it comes to dyslexic students, the brain's academic operating system is clearly not up to the task of the school's demanding academic environment. Reading plays heavily into a healthy operating system, and this system will have to be strengthened. (Strategies for doing so are discussed in Chapter 2 and the next section of this chapter.) Do not get sidetracked in pursuing your plan. Here are the essentials:

1. Believe that it will work; know that the brain can and will change with appropriate interventions.
2. Build a team, and make a plan so that every person is on the same page.
3. Focus on building the operating system. In this case, focus on every part of the system, including processing (typically auditory processing), phonemic awareness, memory, sequencing, attentional skills, fluency, vocabulary, and text comprehension.
4. Always maintain relationships throughout the process.
5. Be positive and patient. This will take time.

Only a qualified reading specialist, neuropsychologist, or certified special education teacher can make a diagnosis of dyslexia. Instruments may include the Woodcock Reading Mastery Test, but that is not sufficient by itself. Since there is no one standard test for dyslexia, the diagnosis is often made by comparing reading ability with IQ and grade-level reading expectations.

Remember that no two people with dyslexia are alike. The only common themes are that these readers struggle. Some enjoy reading, while others do not. Most commonly, they have phonological processing difficulties such as phonemic awareness. Some have greater visual problems (e.g., poor tracking, letters moving). Still others have word memory problems—they cannot recall even the first part of the sentence, much less remember the word's meaning.

Teach literacy at all levels, not just between kindergarten and second grade. Despite mandates in many districts to provide literacy training for educators, most teachers simply don't emphasize literacy skills. The reasons for this include lack of awareness about the extent of the problem, lack of training or motivation, and lack of perceived time in response to high-stakes testing pressures.

Dyslexia is not a disease, nor will medication curb or cure it. Rather, dyslexia is the result of a different style of thinking and learning, and it is best addressed through educational counseling, retraining the brain, behavior modification, and tutoring. Unfortunately, no one strategy works for everyone, and experience tells us that treating dyslexia with a cookie-cutter approach is ineffective. Nevertheless, many educators report having success with a balanced reading program that combines both holistic/meaning and analytic/phonetic approaches with other activities to improve language development. Other helpful strategies are offered in Table 13.2.

Be on the lookout for literacy skills at an early age. Here are a few symptoms to watch for at various levels:

- *Ages 3 and 4:* Look for kids who have trouble holding a book and telling the difference between letters and other symbols. Also note if they can't recognize their name.
- *Kindergarten:* Look for kids who cannot distinguish the sound parts of words like *huh-ahh-tuh* for *hat.* Also, a small vocabulary is a warning sign.

Table 13.2 Potential Solutions and Strategies for Dyslexia

Solutions

- High-interest reading material
- Learning phoneme and symbol correspondences
- Frequent feedback
- Practice at blending and segmenting phonemes in words
- Practice 30 to 90 minutes a day, three to six days a week
- Copy and write spoken words, phrases, and sentences
- Practice reading every day

Strategies

- For high-interest reading material, use personal life stories
- For phonics, use animated literacy and cued articulation
- For phonemic awareness, make short recordings and send home so that there are no mistakes
- Pair good readers with poor readers. The good reader reads the passage, then the poor reader reads the same passage. Each debriefs each other.

- *Grades 1 and 2:* At this age, students might complain that reading is easier for others; they avoid reading; they cannot sound out or do not try to sound out new words.
- *Grades 2 and 3:* At this age, students with dyslexia will make random, wild guesses at words; they will have to try hard at decoding, and often meaning is lost, so they avoid reading.

Start early and be persistent. Remedial action in response to reading difficulties should involve intensive individualized tutoring as early as possible. Phonemic awareness games and programs are especially important at the preK through third-grade levels. Dr. Seuss books, which feature rhyming schemes, are great for enhancing phonemic awareness in the early grades. Some schools have experienced a jump in reading scores that may be related to an increase in rhyming and song games. Fun language games such as Pig Latin (pronounced *ig-pay atin-lay*) may help students develop greater sound awareness, which ultimately impacts reading. Consider the following age-appropriate reading tips:

PreK

- Read all books aloud.
- Use rhyming material.
- Teach songs with simple words.
- Write down children's spoken words.
- Avoid drudgery assignments (e.g., workbooks).

Kindergarten

- Continue to read aloud.
- Emphasize songs, noting especially the words.
- Continue to read rhyming material.
- Evaluate hearing and vision.
- Read enjoyable material (books that are meaningful and fun for learners).
- Keep your eyes and ears open for problems.

Grades 1 and 2

- Read, read, and read more.
- Provide phonemic-awareness testing for all students.
- Balance phonics-based approaches with whole-language reading programs.
- Keep your eyes and ears open for problems.

Grade 3

- Continue reading.
- Request testing if a child exhibits a dislike of reading.
- Keep your eyes and ears open for problems.

Secondary Level

- Teach a three-tier reading process that consists of scanning, organizing, and discussion. (Prereading and scanning help students grasp necessary background information.)
- Provide a list of reading questions to help learners focus and increase comprehension.
- Have learners read small chunks of material and create their own questions or reword yours.
- Ask some "what if" questions to encourage deeper analysis and critical thinking skills.
- Encourage learners to do postreading, review, and discussion of the reading matter.

Accommodate those with dyslexia with the gift of more time—it's fundamental. Other options include advance vocabulary exposure, books on tape, prereading time, being paired up with a partner to work on projects, and extra repetition.

Provide Early Solutions in Vocabulary

Readers need to be exposed to new words as well as to retain them in memory. Vocabulary can be learned both implicitly and explicitly. Teach vocabulary from a variety of directions—verbal, visual, and auditory. Most students learn new vocabulary from oral language usage, read-aloud activities, and extensive reading on their own. The best strategies include preteaching key words, insisting on usage and application, and repeating the words in multiple contexts.

Consider Phonological-Awareness Training

Many people with dyslexia cannot process phonemes fast enough to make sense of them in time before another word comes at them. Phonological processing programs have helped many improve this skill set (Temple et al., 2003). Phonological awareness, a key factor in some reading problems, is addressed by a number of commercial training programs, including Accelerated Reader, Earobics, FastForWord, Lexia, Starfall, Lindamood-Bell, and StudyDog. Such programs ask readers to identify the feel of the sounds they read (e.g., "P is a lip popper."). This approach aims to help learners more clearly distinguish the phonemes of words. Its effectiveness is probably related to its ability to get to the core of the problem—specific word distinctions and sounds needed for linking up seeing and hearing with comprehension. Reading programs in general should address phonological awareness, but students with dyslexia need more of it more often. None of these programs are cheap, and all require staff support. Customized programs are also prevalent and are often used by school speech and hearing therapists.

Reading intervention changes and enhances brain activity to support improved reading after 12 weeks. For reading success, be sure every skill is chunked. Phonemic awareness is auditory and does not involve seeing words in print, so it can be taught by a parent or teacher anytime and anywhere. When you add the blending and segmentation, students learn to combine sounds (*d* and *og* to get *dog*). Phonemic awareness refers to the student's understanding that spoken words and syllables are made up of a sequence of elementary speech sounds. This process can be assessed in students using standardized measures (e.g., Dynamic Indicators of Basic Early Literacy Skills) that offer indices for phonological awareness, alphabetic principle, fluency with connected text, vocabulary, and comprehension.

Be sure to also teach phonemic awareness directly in kindergarten, and teach it explicitly through highlighted sentence structures with playful repetition. Single speech sound-spellings are represented by each letter or letter combination. Provide practice in recognizing these speech sound-spelling relationships in decodable text. Progress from easier to more difficult. Provide practice reading them daily, first in isolation and then in the context of words and sentences. Teach students how to directly sound out words. Do this by blending the words' speech sound-spellings together sequentially from left to right. Then provide practice using words composed of only those speech sound-spelling relationships that have been systematically taught.

Recognize Look-Alike Conditions

Many who struggle with reading may have other issues that mask, exacerbate, or appear to be the real problem. Those other conditions include central auditory processing disorder, sensory integration disorder, or even ADD. In a society that values reading highly, having dyslexia can be very difficult on youngsters. The following can develop as a result of the disorder:

- academic issues (falling behind)
- social issues (being made fun of)
- emotional issues (low self-esteem)

Be prepared and keep eyes and ears tuned into the responses of your students.

Provide Vision Therapy

A small percentage of those with dyslexia have a strong visual, not phonological, deficit. For these readers, combined eye-hand and vestibular training is effective (Reynolds, Nicolson, & Hambly, 2003), and there is evidence that building their visual-spatial skills can pay off (Vidyasagar, 2005). Colored transparencies or Irlen lenses have been shown to help some readers, and in one study, colored contact lenses helped students with dyslexia improve reading speed by 15 percent over the control group (Harris & MacRow-Hill, 1999).

Develop Interventions

Before starting any new reading program, explore alternative sources for the problem (e.g., vision, stress, hearing, home life). Get thorough testing and a complete diagnosis. Create a targeted literacy plan with the individualized education plan team. Collect and align a team, and identify resources. Table 13.3 outlines numerous solutions and strategies for dealing with students who have dyslexia.

Table 13.3   Best Practices and Strategies for Teaching Students With Dyslexia

Phonemic Awareness	<ul><li>Learns in 20 to 50 hours of explicit instruction and exposure to one to five new words</li><li>Must be taught explicitly</li><li>Build these skills:<ul><li>identifying phonemes</li><li>grouping phonemes</li><li>blending phonemes into words</li><li>segmenting words into phonemes</li><li>deleting/adding/substituting phonemes to make words</li></ul></li></ul>
Phonics Instruction	<ul><li>Explicit, systematic instruction works best</li><li>Most effective program when started in kindergarten to first grade</li><li>Build the say-see-say relationships</li><li>Use skill-building model</li></ul>

Fluency Instruction	• Provide high-interest reading material • Use teacher modeling, discussion, and instruments (e.g., tutoring, audiotapes, peer guidance, choral reading, round-robin reading, practice with partners)
Vocabulary Instruction	• Oral language usage • Read-aloud activities • Extensive reading at home • Preteach key words • Insist that students use the words in class • Repeated exposures in multiple contexts • Use audio recordings
Text Comprehension	• Monitor comprehension • Use graphic organizers • Have students generate and answer questions, learn story structures, summarize, and practice prediction • Use of prior knowledge • Metathinking

REVISITING THE STUDENT

"Lee," one of the learners introduced in the pretest at the front of the book, is the student who fits the profile for dyslexia. Like the others, Lee is unique—he exhibits a pattern of symptoms that are associated with a specific disorder. However, some of these symptoms can be observed in other conditions as well. This is why you want to look for patterns rather than isolated behaviors. To help you remember what's important in assessing students with dyslexia, take a moment, relax, and focus on the photo, the symptoms, and the key points of this chapter.

Symptoms

- Has trouble with sequencing, prioritizing, and completing tasks
- Takes spoken or written language literally
- Has difficulty following oral directions and remembering them
- Inability to rhyme by age four
- Confuses left and right, over and under, before and after, and other directional words and concepts
- Lack of dominant handedness; switches hands between or even during tasks
- Unable to correctly complete phonemic awareness tasks
- Has difficulty learning the names and sounds of letters and writing them in alphabetical order

SUPPLEMENTAL RESOURCES

Books/Journals

Annals of Dyslexia

Beyond Dyslexia, by Dorothy Van Den Honert

The Discovery of Cerebellar-Vestibular Syndromes and Therapies, by Harold Levinson

Dyslexia: Practical and Easy-to-Follow Advice, by Robin Temple

Journal of Learning Disabilities

Learning to Read, edited by Laurence Rieben and Charles Perfetti

Overcoming Dyslexia, by Sally Shaywitz

Reversals: A Personal Account of Victory Over Dyslexia, by Eileen M. Simpson

Smart But Feeling Dumb, by Harold Levinson

To Read or Not to Read, by Daphne M. Hurford

Turning Around Upside-Down Kids, by Harold Levinson

Web sites

Bright Solutions for Dyslexia: www.dys-add.com

Davis Dyslexia Association International: www.dyslexia.com

Dyslexia Institutes of America: www.dyslexiainstitutes.com

International Dyslexia Association: www.interdys.org

Learning Disabilities Association of America: www.ldanatl.org

National Center for Learning Disabilities: www.ncld.org

Scientific Learning: www.scilearn.com

University of Buffalo, School of Medicine and Biomedical Sciences: www.smbs.buffalo.edu

Posttest

CAN YOU IDENTIFY THESE LEARNERS?

Learner No. 1: Miguel

Symptoms

◆ Loses his temper often
◆ Argues with adults; defies authority and rejects adults' requests or rules; complies about 10 to 20 percent of the time
◆ Deliberately annoys others and is easily annoyed himself
◆ Blames others for his own mistakes or misbehavior
◆ Angry and resentful; vindictive for no apparent reason
◆ Swears and uses obscene language

What's most likely going on?

Answer: Oppositional Defiant Disorder

Learner No. 2: Tom

Symptoms

◆ Displays a high level of apathy, listlessness, or lack of vigor
◆ Passive and unresponsive in spite of shocking or surprising events
◆ Does not initiate new activities or learning
◆ Does not feel in control of his environment; likely to say, "What's the point?," "Why bother?," "Who cares?," or "So what?"
◆ Lack of hostility even when hostility is warranted
◆ Increased sarcasm

What's most likely going on?

Answer: Learned Helplessness

Learner No. 3: Joshua

Symptoms

- Inappropriate emotional outbursts with random acts of destruction
- Consistently hurtful toward peers—swatting, hitting, and verbal intimidation
- Refuses to follow directions directly; consistently challenges authority
- Loud and aggressive communication patterns, often taunting the teacher and using vulgar language
- Unwilling to participate with others in normal social activities
- Is prone to lie

What's most likely going on?

Answer: Conduct Disorder

Learner No. 4: Mary

Symptoms

- Seems to be edgy and on alert
- Trance-like state is common; doesn't snap out of it quickly
- Appears bored and disconnected
- Short-term memory loss and inability to prioritize
- Makes careless errors in her work
- Decreased social contact
- Doesn't remember "where" questions
- Loss of creativity and poor concentration
- Seems to be sick more often than peers

What's most likely going on?

Answer: Stress Disorder

Learner No. 5: Michelle

Symptoms

◆ Decrease in energy
◆ Change in appetite and subsequent weight loss or gain
◆ Feelings of worthlessness and guilt
◆ Inability to think clearly or concentrate; indecisiveness
◆ Angry, sometimes suicidal imaginings
◆ Persistent sad, anxious, or empty mood
◆ Feelings of hopelessness; pessimism
◆ Loss of interest or pleasure in ordinary activities or hobbies
◆ Restlessness, irritability, unexplained aches and pains
◆ Unusual loss of friends; reduction in academic performance

What's most likely going on?

Answer: Depression

Learner No. 6: Robert

Symptoms

◆ Stays to himself
◆ Often gets stuck and repeats behaviors
◆ Seems obsessed with details
◆ Dislikes changes of routines or surprises
◆ Makes little or no eye contact
◆ Gets sick more often than others
◆ Misses the big picture
◆ Shows fascination over apparent trivia

What's most likely going on?

Answer: Pervasive Developmental Disorder

Learner No. 7: Ashley

Symptoms

- Difficulty structuring work time
- Impaired rates of learning and poor memory
- Has trouble generalizing behaviors and information
- Sometimes exhibits impulsive behavior
- Easily distracted and frequently exhibits reduced attention span
- Displays a sense of fearlessness; is unresponsive to verbal cautions
- Displays poor social judgment
- Has trouble internalizing modeled behaviors
- Language production is higher than comprehension
- Overall poor problem-solving strategies
- May have unusual facial features

What's most likely going on?

Answer: Learning Delayed

Learner No. 8: Courtney

Symptoms

- Has difficulty with number and order sequences
- Understands the importance of working left to right
- Finds telling the time on an analogue clock difficult
- Scatters tally marks instead of organizing them systematically
- Gets confused with division (e.g., is it 3 into 6, or 6 into 3?)
- Gets easily overloaded by pages/worksheets full of figures
- Makes copies of work/shapes inaccurately

What's most likely going on?

Answer: Dyscalculia

Learner No. 9: Brent

Symptoms

◆ Inattentive to others
◆ Easily distracted
◆ Engages in a lot of head turning to hear better
◆ Retrieval problems ("Um. . . . I forget the word.")
◆ Difficulty following oral directions
◆ Omits word endings
◆ Speaks words out of order
◆ Mistaken words—says "starvation army" instead of Salvation Army or "fum" instead of thumb

What's most likely going on?

Answer: Central Auditory Processing Disorder

Learner No. 10: Jason

Symptoms

◆ Rarely finishes his work
◆ Calls out answers in class; never waits his turn
◆ Easily and consistently distracted
◆ Exhibits weak follow-through and preparation for future events
◆ Wants everything right away; has no patience
◆ Personal area (desk) is a mess
◆ Doesn't seem able to reflect on the past in order to learn from it
◆ Doesn't sit still; always on the go
◆ Can't hold several thoughts at a time
◆ Hindsight or foresight rarely evident

What's most likely going on?

Answer: Attention Deficit Hyperactivity Disorder

Learner No. 11: Lee

Symptoms

- Has trouble with sequencing, prioritizing, and completing tasks
- Takes spoken or written language literally
- Has difficulty following oral directions and remembering them
- Inability to rhyme by age four
- Confuses left and right, over and under, before and after, and other directionality words and concepts
- Lack of dominant handedness; switches hands between or even during tasks
- Unable to correctly complete phonemic awareness tasks
- Has difficulty learning the names and sounds of letters and writing them in alphabetical order

What's most likely going on?

Answer: Dyslexia

CONGRATULATIONS!

References

Ackerman, P. T., Newton, J. E., McPherson, W. B., Jones, J. G., & Dykman, R. A. (1998). Prevalence of post traumatic stress disorder and other psychiatric diagnoses in three groups of abused children (sexual, physical, and both). *Child Abuse and Neglect, 22,* 759–774.

American Psychiatric Association. (2000). *Diagnostic and statistical manual of mental disorders* (4th ed., text revision). Washington, DC: Author.

Ansari, D. (2008). Effects of development and enculturation on number representation in the brain. *Nature Reviews Neuroscience, 9,* 278–291.

Baker, J. P. (2008). Mercury, vaccines, and autism: One controversy, three histories. *American Journal of Public Health, 98*(2), 244–253.

Barkley, R. A. (2002). International consensus statement on ADHD: January 2002. *Clinical Child and Family Psychology Review, 5,* 89–111.

Benton, D. (2007). The impact of diet on anti-social, violent and criminal behaviour. *Neuroscience and Biobehavioral Reviews, 31,* 752–774.

Benton, D., & Donohoe, R. T. (1999). The effects of nutrients on mood. *Public Health Nutrition, 2,* 403–409.

Bertrand, J., Mars, A., Boyle, C., Bove, F., Yeargin-Allsopp, M., & Decoufle, P. (2001). Prevalence of autism in a United States population: The Brick Township, New Jersey, investigation. *Pediatrics, 108,* 1155–1561.

Biederman, J., Faraone, S. V., & Monuteaux, M. C. (2002). Differential effect of environmental adversity by gender: Rutter's index of adversity in a group of boys and girls with and without ADHD. *American Journal of Psychiatry, 159,* 1556–1562.

Brown, S. M., Henning, S., & Wellman, C. L. (2005). Mild, short-term stress alters dendritic morphology in rat medial prefrontal cortex. *Cerebral Cortex, 15,* 1714–1722.

Butterworth, B. (1999). *The mathematical brain.* London: Macmillan.

Butterworth, B. (2003). *Dyscalculia screener.* London: nferNelson.

Cage, B., & Smith, J. (2000). The effects of chess instruction on mathematics achievement of southern, rural, black secondary students. *Research in the Schools, 7*(1), 19–26.

Campbell, S. B., Spieker, S., Burchinal, M., Poe, M. D., & The NICHD Early Child Care Research Network. (2006). Trajectories of aggression from toddlerhood to age 9 predict academic and social functioning through age 12. *Journal of Child Psychology and Psychiatry, and Allied Disciplines, 47*(8), 791–800.

Castellanos, F. X., & Acosta, M. T. (2004). The neuroanatomy of attention deficit/hyperactivity disorder. *Revista de Neurologia, 38*(Suppl. 1), S131–S136.

Chaouloff, F. (1989). Physical exercise and brain monoamines: A review. *Acta Physiologica Scandinavica, 137,* 1–13.

Charlop-Christy, M. H., Carpenter, M., Le, L., LeBlanc, L. A., & Kellet, K. (2002). Using the picture exchange communication system (PECS) with children with autism: Assessment of PECS acquisition, speech, social-communicative behavior, and problem behavior. *Journal of Applied Behavior Analysis, 35,* 213–231.

Cherkassky, V. L., Kana, R. K., Keller, T. A., & Just, M. A. (2006). Functional connectivity in a baseline resting-state network in autism. *NeuroReport, 17,* 1687–1690.

Christakis, D. A., & Wright, J. A. (2004). Can continuity of care be improved? Results from a randomized pilot study. *Ambulatory Pediatrics, 4,* 336–339.

Chugani, H. T., Juhász, C., Behen, M. E., Ondersma, R., & Muzik, O. (2007). Autism with facial port-wine stain: A new syndrome? *Pediatric Neurology, 37,* 192–199.

Clarke, H. F., Dalley, J. W., Crofts, H. S., Robbins, T. W., & Roberts, A. C. (2004). Cognitive inflexibility after prefrontal serotonin depletion. *Science, 304,* 878–880.

Clausen-May, T., Claydon, H., & Ruddock, G. (1999). *Mental mathematics 6–14 test series.* Windsor, England: nferNelson.

Covassin, T., Stearne, D., & Elbin, R., III. (2008). Concussion history and postconcussion neurocognitive performance and symptoms in collegiate athletes. *Journal of Athletic Training, 43,* 119–124.

Davis, C. J., Knopik, V. S., Wadsworth, S. J., & DeFries, J. C. (2000). Self-reported reading problems in parents of twins with reading difficulties. *Twin Res, 3*(2), 88–91.

Dervic, K., Gould, M. S., Lenz, G., Kleinman, M., Akkaya-Kalayci, T., Velting, D., et al. (2006). Youth suicide risk factors and attitudes in New York and Vienna: A cross-cultural comparison. *Suicide Life-Threatening Behavior, 36,* 539–552.

Ding, Y. C., Chi, H. C., Grady, D. L., Morishima, A., Kidd, J. R., Kidd, K. K., et al. (2000). Evidence of positive selection acting at the human dopamine receptor D4 gene locus. *Proceedings of the National Academy of Sciences, 99*(1), 309–314.

Dowker, A. (2003). Brain-based research on arithmetic: Implications for learning and teaching. In I. Thompson (Ed.), *Enhancing primary mathematics teaching* (pp. 191–198). Maidenhead, England: Open University Press.

Durston, S. (2003). A review of the biological bases of ADHD: What have we learned from imaging studies? *Mental Retardation and Developmental Disabilities Research Reviews, 9,* 184–195.

Elgar, K., & Campbell, R. (2001). The cognitive neuroscience of face recognition: Implications for developmental disorders. *Journal of Child Psychology, Psychiatry, and Allied Disciplines, 42,* 705–717.

Emery, R. E., & Laumann-Billings, L. (1998). An overview of the nature, causes, and consequences of abusive family relationships: Toward differentiating maltreatment and violence. *American Psychologist, 53,* 121–135.

Erickson, K., Drevets, W., & Schulkin, J. (2003). Glucocorticoid regulation of diverse cognitive functions in normal and pathological emotional states. *Neuroscience Biobehavioral Review, 27,* 233–246.

Evans, G. W., Gonnella, C., Marcynyszyn, L. A., Gentile, L., & Salpekar, N. (2005). The role of chaos in poverty and children's socioemotional adjustment. *Psychological Science, 16*(7), 560–565.

Federman, M., Garner, T. I., Short, K., Cutter, W. B. C., IV, Kiely, J., Levine, D., et al. (1996). What does it mean to be poor in America? *Monthly Labor Review, 119*(5), 3–17.

Feigenson, L., Dehaene, S., & Spelke, E. (2004). Core systems of number. *Trends in Cognitive Science, 8,* 307–314.

Fisher, S. E., & DeFries, J. C. (2002). Developmental dyslexia: Genetic dissection of a complex cognitive trait. *Nature Reviews Neuroscience, 3,* 767–780.

Fox, M., Pac, S., Devaney, B., & Jankowski, L. (2004). Feeding infants and toddlers study: What foods are infants and toddlers eating? *Journal of the American Dietetic Association, 104,* 22–30.

Galaburda, A. M. (1993). Neuroanatomic basis of developmental dyslexia. *Clinical Neurology and Neurosurgery, 11,* 161–173.

Geary, D. C. (1999). *Mathematical disabilities: What we know and don't know.* Retrieved May 24, 2009, from http://www.ldonline.org/article/Mathematical_Disabilities:__What_We_Know_and_Don't_Know

González-Tejera, G., Canino, G., Ramírez, R., Chávez, L., Shrout, P., Bird, H., et al. (2005). Examining minor and major depression in adolescents. *Journal of Child Psychology and Psychiatry, 46,* 888–899.

Grossberg, S., & Seidman, D. (2006). Neural dynamics of autistic behaviors: Cognitive, emotional, and timing substrates. *Psychological Review, 113,* 483–525.

Guillette, E. A., Meza, M. M., Aquilar, M. G., Soto, A. D., & Garcia, I. E. (1998). An anthropological approach to the evaluation of preschool children exposed to pesticides in Mexico. *Environmental Health Perspectives, 106*(6), 347–353.

Habib, M. (2000). The neurological basis of developmental dyslexia: An overview and working hypothesis. *Brain, 123*(12), 2373–2399.

Hainsworth, T. (2006). The prevalence and causes of autistic spectrum disorders. *Nursing Times, 102*(31), 23–24.

Harding, K. L., Judah, R. D., & Gant, C. (2003). Outcome-based comparison of Ritalin versus food-supplement treated children with AD/HD. *Alternative Medicine Review, 8,* 319–330.

Harris, D., & MacRow-Hill, S. J. (1999). Application of ChromaGen haploscopic lenses to patients with dyslexia: A double-masked, placebo-controlled trial. *Journal of the American Optometric Association, 70,* 629–640.

Herbert, M. R., Russo, J. P., Yang, S., Roohi, J., Blaxill, M., Kahler, S. G., et al. (2006). Autism and environmental genomics. *Neurotoxicology, 27,* 671–684.

Huttenlocher, J., Vasilyeva, M., Cymerman, E., & Levine, S. (2002). Language input and child syntax. *Cognitive Psychology, 45*(3), 337–374.

Isaacs, E. B., Edmonds, C. J., Lucas, A., & Gadian, D. G. (2001). Calculation difficulties in children of very low birthweight: A neural correlate. *Brain, 124,* 1701–1707.

Iuculano, T., Tang, J., Hall, C. W., & Butterworth, B. (2008). Core information processing deficits in developmental dyscalculia and low numeracy. *Developmental Science, 11,* 669–680.

Jacobson, M. F. (1996). Effects of sugar on behavior in children. *Journal of the American Medical Association, 275,* 756–757.

James, W. H. (2008). Further evidence that some male-based neurodevelopmental disorders are associated with high intrauterine testosterone concentrations. *Developmental Medicine and Child Neurology, 50,* 15–18.

Jensen, P. S., Hinshaw, S. P., Swanson, J. M., Greenhill, L. L., Conners, C. K., Arnold, L. E., et al. (2001). Findings from the NIMH Multimodal Treatment Study of ADHD (MTA): Implications and applications for primary care providers. *Journal of Developmental and Behavioral Pediatrics, 22,* 60–73.

Kerns, K. A., McInerney, R. J., & Wilde, N. J. (2001). Time reproduction, working memory, and behavioral inhibition in children with ADHD. *Child Neuropsychology, 7,* 21–31.

Kieling, C., Goncalves, R. R., Tannock, R., & Castellanos, F. X. (2008). Neurobiology of attention deficit hyperactivity disorder. *Child and Adolescent Psychiatric Clinics of North America, 17*(2), 285–307.

King, J. A., Abend, S., & Edwards, E. (2001). Genetic predisposition and the development of posttraumatic stress disorder in an animal model. *Biological Psychiatry, 50,* 231–237.

Knickmeyer, R., Baron-Cohen, S., Raggatt, P., & Taylor, K. (2005). Foetal testosterone, social relationships, and restricted interests in children. *Journal of Child Psychology and Psychiatry, 46,* 198–210.

Koegel, R. L., Bimbela, A., & Schreibman, L. (1996). Collateral effects of parent training on family interactions. *Journal of Autism Developmental Disorders, 26,* 347–359.

Kollins, S. H., McClernon, F. J., & Fuemmeler, B. F. (2005). Association between smoking and attention-deficit/hyperactivity disorder symptoms in a population-based sample of young adults. *Archives of General Psychiatry, 62,* 1142–1147.

Kondo, H., Osaka, N., & Osaka, M. (2005). Cooperation of the anterior cingulate cortex and dorsolateral prefrontal cortex for attention shifting. *Neuroimage, 23,* 670–679.

Lavigne, J. V., Cicchetti, C., Gibbons, R. D., Binns, H. J., Larsen, L., & DeVito, C. (2001). Oppositional defiant disorder with onset in preschool years: Longitudinal stability and pathways to other disorders. *Journal of the American Academy of Child and Adolescent Psychiatry, 40,* 1393–1400.

Lemer, C., Dehaene, S., Spelke, E., & Cohen, L. (2003). Approximate quantities and exact number words: Dissociable systems. *Neuropsychologia, 41,* 1942–1958.

Lewinsohn, P. M., Rohde, P., & Seeley, J. R. (1998). Treatment of adolescent depression: Frequency of services and impact on functioning in young adulthood. *Depression and Anxiety, 7,* 47–52.

Liu, Q. J., Ma, F., Li, D., Wang, X. W., Tian, W. Y., Chen, Y., et al. (2005). Detection of chromosome aberrations in Chinese children with autism using G-banding and BAC FISH. *Zhonghua Yi Xue Yi Chuan Xue Za Zhi, 22,* 254–257.

Lou, H. C., Rosa, P., Pryds, O., Karrebaek, H., Lunding, J., Cumming, P., & Gjedde, A. (2004). ADHD: Increased dopamine receptor availability linked to attention deficit and low neonatal cerebral blood flow. *Developmental Medicine & Child Neurology, 46*(3), 179–183.

Lupien, S. J., McEwan, B. S., Gunnar, M. R., & Heim, C. (2009, April 29). Effects of stress throughout the lifespan on the brain, behaviour and cognition. *Nature Reviews Neuroscience.* (published online ahead of print)

Margulies, S. (1991). *The effect of chess on reading scores.* New York: American Chess Federation.

Maulik, P. K., & Darmstadt, G. L. (2009, April 30). Community-based interventions to optimize early childhood development in low resource settings. *Journal of Perinatology.* (published online ahead of print)

Mazziotta, J. C., Woods, R., Iacoboni, M., Sicotte, N., Yaden, K., Tran, M., et al. (2009). The myth of the normal, average human brain—The ICBM experience: (1) Subject screening and eligibility. *Neuroimage, 44,* 914–922.

McEwen, B. S. (2008). Central effects of stress hormones in health and disease: Understanding the protective and damaging effects of stress and stress mediators. *European Journal of Pharmacology, 583,* 174–185.

Molko, N., Cachia, A., Rivière, D., Mangin, J. F., Bruandet, M., Le Bihan, D., et al. (2003). Functional and structural alterations of the intraparietal sulcus in a developmental dyscalculia of genetic origin. *Neuron, 40,* 847–858.

Morrison, J. (1995). *DSM-IV made easy: The clinician's guide to diagnosis.* New York: Guilford Press.

Nabkasorn, C., Miyai, N., Sootmongkol, A., Junprasert, S., Yamamoto, H., Arita, M., et al. (2006). Effects of physical exercise on depression, neuroendocrine stress hormones and physiological fitness in adolescent females with depressive symptoms. *European Journal of Public Health, 16,* 179–184.

National Institute of Mental Health. (1996). *Attention deficit hyperactivity disorder: Decade of the brain* (Report No. 96–3572). Bethesda, MD: Author.

Osman, B. B. (2000). *Learning disabilities and the risk of psychiatric disorders in children and adolescents.* Washington, DC: American Psychiatric Association.

Passik, S. D., & Kirsh, K. L. (2006). Fear and loathing in the pain clinic. *Pain Medicine, 7,* 363–364.

Pastor, P. N., & Reuben, C. A. (2005). Racial and ethnic differences in ADHD and LD in young school-age children: Parental reports in the National Health Interview Survey. *Public Health Reports, 120*(4), 383–392.

Paulesu, E., Frith, U., Snowling, M., Gallagher, A., Morton, J., Frackowiak, R. S. J., et al. (1996). Is developmental dyslexia a disconnection syndrome? Evidence from PET scanning. *Brain, 119,* 143–157.

Pavone, P., Incorpora, G., Fiumara, A., Parano, E., Trifiletti, R. R., & Ruggieri, M. (2004). Epilepsy is not a prominent feature of primary autism. *Neuropediatrics, 35,* 207–210.

Pennington, L., James, P., McNally, R., Pay, H., & McConachie, H. (2009). Analysis of compositional data in communication disorders research. *Journal of Communication Disorders, 42,* 18–28.

Pereira, A. C., Huddleston, D. E., Brickman, A. M., Sosunov, A. A., Hen, R., McKhann, G. M., et al. (2007). An *in vivo* correlate of exercise-induced neurogenesis in the adult dentate gyrus. *Proceedings of the National Academy of Sciences of the United States of America, 104,* 5638–5643.

Perry, B. D., & Pollard, R. (1997). *Altered brain development following global neglect in early childhood.* Proceedings from the annual meeting of the Society for Neuroscience, New Orleans, LA.

Poeppel, D., Guillemin, A., Thompson, J., Fritz, J., Bavelier, D., & Braun, A. R. (2004). Auditory lexical decision, categorical perception, and FM direction discrimination differentially engage left and right auditory cortex. *Neuropsychologia, 42,* 183–200.

Posner, M., Rothbart, M. K., Sheese, B. E., & Kieras, J. (2008). How arts training influences cognition. In C. Asbury & B. Rich (Eds.), *Learning, arts, and the brain: The Dana Consortium report on arts and cognition* (pp. 1–10). New York: Dana Press.

Reynolds, D., Nicolson, R. I., & Hambly, H. (2003). Evaluation of an exercise-based treatment for children with reading difficulties. *Dyslexia, 9,* 48–71.

Riccio, C. A., Amado, A., Jiménez, S., Hasbrouk, J. E., Imhoff, B., & Denton, C. (2001). Cross-linguistic transfer of phonological processing: Development of a measure of phonological processing in Spanish. *Bilingual Research Journal, 25,* 417–437.

Rice, D., & Barone, S., Jr. (2000). Critical periods of vulnerability for the developing nervous system: Evidence from humans and animal models. *Environmental Health Perspectives, 108*(Suppl. 3), 511–533.

Richards, T. L., & Berninger, V. W. (2008). Abnormal fMRI connectivity in children with dyslexia during a phoneme task: Before but not after treatment 1. *Journal of Neurolinguistics, 21,* 294–304.

Ridley, R. M. (1994). The psychology of perserverative and stereotyped behaviour. *Progress in Neurobiology, 44,* 221–231.

Rosen, S. (2005). "A riddle wrapped in a mystery inside an enigma": Defining central auditory processing disorder. *American Journal of Audiology, 14*(2), 139–150.

Rossi, E. (2002). *The psychobiology of gene expression.* New York: W. W. Norton.

Salend, S. J., & Rohena, E. (2003). Students with attention deficit disorders: An overview. *Intervention in School and Clinic, 38,* 259–266.

Sallows, G. O., & Graupner, T. D. (2005). Intensive behavioral treatment for children with autism: Four-year outcome and predictors. *American Journal of Mental Retardation, 110,* 417–438.

Sands, S. A., Strong, R., Corbitt, J., & Morilak, D. A. (2000). Effects of acute restraint stress on tyrosine hydroxylase mRNA expression in locus coeruleus of Wistar and Wistar-Kyoto rats. *Brain Res Mol Brain Res, 75*(1), 1–7.

Scahill, L. (2005). Diagnosis and evaluation of pervasive developmental disorders. *Journal of Clinical Psychiatry, 66*(Suppl. 10), 19–25.

Schaefer, G. B., Mendelsohn, N. J., & Professional Practice and Guidelines Committee. (2008). Clinical genetics evaluation in identifying the etiology of autism spectrum disorders. *Genetics in Medicine, 10,* 301–305.

Schnurr, P. P., Friedman, M. J., Foy, D. W., Shea, M. T., Hsieh, F. Y., Lavori, P. W., et al. (2003). Randomized trial of trauma-focused group therapy for posttraumatic stress disorder: Results from a Department of Veterans Affairs cooperative study. *Archives of General Psychiatry, 60,* 481–489.

Seligman, M. (1998). *Learned optimism.* New York: Pocket Books.

Seligman, M. L. (2006). *Learned optimism: How to change your mind and your life.* New York: Vintage Press.

Shalev, R. S., & Gross-Tsur, V. (2001). Developmental dyscalculia. *Pediatric Neurology, 24,* 337–342.

Shaywitz, B. A., Skudlarski, P., Holahan, J. M., Marchione, K. E., Constable, R. T., Fulbright, R. K., et al. (2007). Age-related changes in reading systems of dyslexic children. *Annals of Neurology, 61,* 363–370.

Singh, H., & O'Boyle, M. W. (2004). Interhemispheric interaction during global-local processing in mathematically gifted adolescents, average-ability youth, and college students. *Neuropsychology, 18,* 371–377.

Slomine, B. S., Salorio, C. F., Grados, M. A., Vasa, R. A., Christensen, J. R., & Gerring, J. P. (2005). Differences in attention, executive functioning, and memory in children with and without ADHD after severe traumatic brain injury. *Journal of the International Neuropsychological Society, 11,* 645–653.

Southgate, V., & Hamilton, A. F. (2008). Unbroken mirrors: Challenging a theory of autism. *Trends in Cognitive Science, 12,* 225–229.

Steffenburg, S. (1991). Neuropsychiatric assessment of children with autism: A population-based study. *Developmental Medicine and Child Neurology, 33,* 495–511.

Stein, M. B., & Stein, D. J. (2008). Social anxiety disorder. *Lancet, 371,* 1115–1125.

Stella, S. G., Vilar, A. P., Lacroix, C., Fisberg, M., Santos, R. F., Mello, M. T., et al. (2005). Effects of type of physical exercise and leisure activities on the depression scores of obese Brazilian adolescent girls. *Brazilian Journal of Medical and Biological Research, 38,* 1683–1689.

Stone, W. L., McMahon, C. R., Yoder, P. J., & Walden, T. A. (2007). Early social-communicative and cognitive development of younger siblings of children with autism spectrum disorders. *Archives of Pediatrics and Adolescent Medicine, 161*(4), 384–390.

Stotz-Ingenlath, G. (2000). Epistemological aspects of Eugen Bleuler's conception of schizophrenia in 1911. *Medicine, Health Care, and Philosophy, 3,* 153–159.

Temple, E., Deutsch, G. K., Poldrack, R. A., Miller, S. L., Tallal, P., Merzenich, M. M., et al. (2003). Neural deficits in children with dyslexia ameliorated by behavioral remediation: Evidence from functional MRI. *Proceeding of the National Academy of Sciences of the United States of America, 100,* 2860–2865.

Tressoldi, P. E., Rosati, M., & Lucangeli, D. (2007). Patterns of developmental dyscalculia with or without dyslexia. *Neurocase, 13,* 217–225.

Turner, R. J., & Avison, W. R. (2003). Status variations in stress exposure among young adults: Implications for the interpretation of prior research. *Journal of Health and Social Behavior, 44,* 488–505.

U.S. Census Bureau. (2004). Population survey (March Suppl. 2004). Washington, DC: U.S. Government Printing Office.

U.S. Department of Health and Human Services. (1999). *Mental health: A report of the Surgeon General.* Rockville, MD: Author. Retrieved May 12, 2009, from http://www.surgeongeneral.gov/library/mentalhealth/home.html

U.S. Food and Drug Administration (n.d.). Thimerosal in Vaccines Questions and Answers. Retrieved September 8, 2009 from http://www.fda.gov/BiologicsBloodVaccines/Vaccines/QuestionsaboutVaccines/ucm070430.htm

Vidyasagar, T. R. (2005). Attentional gating in primary visual cortex: A physiological basis for dyslexia. *Perception, 34,* 903–911.

Volkow, N. D., Wang, G. J., Fowler, J. S., Logan, J., Franceschi, D., Maynard, L., et al. (2002). Relationship between blockade of dopamine transporters by oral methylphenidate and the increases in extracellular dopamine: Therapeutic implications. *Synapse, 43,* 181–187.

von Aster, M. G., & Shalev, R. S. (2007). Number development and developmental dyscalculia. *Developmental Medicine and Child Neurology, 49,* 868–873.

Weicker, H., & Struder, H. K. (2001). Influence of exercise on serotonergic neuromodulation in the brain. *Amino Acids, 20,* 35–47.

Westerberg, H., & Klingberg, T. (2007). Changes in cortical activity after training of working memory—A single-subject analysis. *Physiology and Behavior, 92,* 186–192.

Yao, Y., Walsh, W. J., McGinnis, W. R., & Pratico, D. (2006). Altered vascular phenotype in autism: Correlation with oxidative stress. *Archives of Neurology, 63,* 1161–1164.

Yücel, M., Harrison, B. J., Wood, S. J., Fornito, A., Clarke, K., Wellard, R. M., et al. (2007). State, trait and biochemical influences on human anterior cingulate function. *Neuroimage, 34,* 1766–1773.

Index

CORWIN

A SAGE Company

The Corwin logo—a raven striding across an open book—represents the union of courage and learning. Corwin is committed to improving education for all learners by publishing books and other professional development resources for those serving the field of PreK–12 education. By providing practical, hands-on materials, Corwin continues to carry out the promise of its motto: **"Helping Educators Do Their Work Better."**